MW00966521

Dating
IRON JOHN
and Other Pleasures

Dating
IRON JOHN
and Other Pleasures

A WOMAN'S SURVIVAL GUIDE
FOR THE '90s

Linda Sunshine

A Birch Lane Press Book
Published by Carol Publishing Group

A Birch Lane Press Book

Published by Carol Publishing Group

Birch Lane Press is a registered trademark of Carol Communications, Inc.

Editorial Offices: 600 Madison Avenue, New York, N.Y. 10022

Sales and Distribution Offices: 120 Enterprise Avenue, Secaucus, N.J. 07094

In Canada: Canadian Manda Group, P.O. Box 920, Station U, Toronto, Ontario M8Z 5P9

Queries regarding rights and permissions should be addressed to Carol Publishing Group, 600 Madison Avenue, New York, N.Y. 10022

Carol Publishing Group books are available at special discounts for bulk purchases, for sales promotions, fund-raising, or educational purposes. Special editions can be created to specifications. For details contact: Special Sales Department, Carol Publishing Group, 120 Enterprise Avenue, Secaucus, N.J. 07094

Special thanks to Meredith Bernstein and Hillel Black

A different version of "Lying Like Leona" appeared as "The (Biggest) Lies You Tell Yourself" in *Cosmopolitan*, November 1992. "Sex Ruins Everything" originally appeared in *New York Woman*, June/July 1991. "You Just Don't Understand Iron John: Communicating with Real Men!" appeared in a slightly different form as "Lexicon of Love," in *Woman*, May 1990.

Manufactured in the United States of America

10   9   8   7   6   5   4   3   2   1

Library of Congress Cataloging-in-Publication Data

Sunshine, Linda.
    Dating Iron John : a woman's survival guide for the '90s / by
  Linda Sunshine
      p.   cm.
    "A Birch Lane Press book."
    ISBN 1-55972-175-8
    ISBN 1–55972–188–X (paper)
    1. Dating (Social customs)—United States.   2. Man-woman
  relationships—United States.   I. Title.
  HQ801.S93   1993
  646.7'—dc20   92-39826
                                                    CIP

To my dear friend, Nancy Diamond, who died this year in a car accident in Italy. Nan and I lived on opposite coasts, so we spent many hours on the phone, late at night, mainly talking about men, love, and relationships. Always supportive and nonjudgmental, Nan encouraged many of the mistakes I made in the past six years.

Still, there's a big empty space in my life since Nan took her permanent vacation. I only hope that wherever she is now, the men are cute, the sex is good, and the relationships are less complicated.

Contents

Dating
IRON JOHN
and Other Pleasures

Always Open With a Joke

There once was a man who had three girlfriends, and he couldn't decide which one to marry. He decided to give five thousand dollars to each woman to see what she would do with it.

The first woman bought new clothes for herself. She got an expensive new hairdo, a massage, a facial, a manicure, and a pedicure. She said, "I spent the money so that I would look pretty for you because I love you so much."

The second woman bought a VCR, a CD player, a set of golf clubs, and a tennis racket and gave them to the man. "I used the money to buy you these gifts because I love you," she told him.

The third woman invested the money in the stock market and within a short time had doubled her investment. She returned the initial five thousand dollars to the man and reinvested the profit. "I'm investing in our future because I love you so much," she said.

The man carefully considered how each woman had spent the money, and married the woman with the big tits.

—Wisecracks

How I Became a Dating Expert

It's a strange twist of fate that I've come to spend so much time writing about relationships. In 1985, I was asked to write a book about dating. I hardly felt qualified at the time since, after ending a six-year relationship with a married man (don't ask!), I hadn't dated in almost two years. In the end, though, I went ahead and wrote *Women Who Date Too Much (And Those Who Should Be So Lucky!)*. Several chapters were excerpted in women's magazines. To promote the book, I went out on a national tour, traveling to various cities to appear on talk shows and give radio interviews. A show in Detroit sent me a tape of my appearance, and watching it, I saw that when I was on camera my name appeared on the screen, and under it was this credential: *Dating Expert*.

Since that day I've often wondered exactly what qualifications went into making me an expert in the field of dating. Yes, I have been dating for a very long time, but I have learned only three general things about the process: Your first love is only target practice, the good-looking guys are never the best lovers, and married men don't leave their wives. Does this make me an expert? It seems to me that if you're an expert at dating, you date yourself into marriage and out of the title.

Romance was difficult enough when *Women Who Date Too Much* was published. Instead of getting better in the 1990s, though, we got Iron John, Clarence Thomas, Mike Tyson, *American Psycho*, William Kennedy Smith, Hannibal Lecter, *Basic Instinct*, Donald Trump, and *Vox*. No wonder relationships between men and women have gone ballistic. "Who wrote the book of love?" we all wonder. "And why are there so many typos?"

Dating Iron John actually began as a proposal about death. A funny book about death that included a lot of stuff about dating and sex. (If you're dating, you'll understand the connection.) According to my agent, there wasn't a real enthusiastic response for the proposal. But one editor who read the manuscript thought that with just the chapters about women and men and sex, I had the foundation for a book about relationships. Again I was asked to write a book about dating, and, again, I was in a nondating mode of life. (This is the cyclical nature of dating so common among single people.)

I didn't want to tell my agent that I hadn't had a date in four months because I was in love with a maniac who made my life hell. The only way I could handle the dilemma was to break up with him and be miserable without him, which was slightly more endurable than being miserable with him, except I really missed the sex. In the end, I used the time afforded me by his absence to write this book and ultimately was grateful to him since our relationship provided material for at least five chapters.

In fact, all of the men I have ever loved (or wanted to love) appear in this book in one form or another. In thinking about these men, I've discovered that all my relationships have two things in common: they all began great and they all ended badly.

You never know when you're going to meet someone and fall in love. This is the great mystery and appeal of staying single. "All things are contingent, and there is chaos," the author Spalding Gray was told by his shrink. I believe the same is true of dating, especially the part about chaos.

As for breaking up, once the relationship is over, you never really know what went wrong; you just feel nauseous whenever the subject comes to mind. After a plane crash there's the black box that tells the FAA what caused the crack-up. Too bad there's no black box of relationships.

Still, I'm a sucker for romance even when it means becoming a victim of unrequited love. I guess I can honestly say that if it weren't for unrequited love, I'd have nothing to write about. And I wouldn't be the dating expert I am today.

Dating Iron John

> Women have become so powerful that our independence has been lost in our homes and is now being trampled and stampeded underfoot in public.
>
> —Cato, 195 B.C.

In the 1970s and early 1980s, men were encouraged to get in touch with the feminine aspects of their personalities. All over the country, women were looking across the breakfast table at their husbands and lovers and asking, "Why can't you be more like Alan Alda or Phil Donahue?"

Alan and Phil represented the ideal men of their day—thoughtful, generous, kind, loving, sensitive, supportive of women's liberation, peace-loving, aware of their emotions, capable and eager to express their true feelings. And they both had great hair.

Attempting to imitate these model icons, many men attended workshops and men's-issue classes. They joined consciousness groups and went into therapy to deal with their innermost emotions. They learned to feel their pain and express their anger in constructive ways. They wore their hearts on their sleeve and their hair in a ponytail.

These sensitive men accepted the premise that women were

equal and began treating them that way. They hired women for executive positions and helped their wives with child care and household chores. But, at the same time, men stopped lighting women's cigarettes, they expected women to carry their own suitcases, and, most disturbingly, they sometimes refused to pay for dinner.

Secretly, women began to doubt that the feminized man was actually an improvement over the old model. By the mid-1980s, both Alan Alda and Phil Donahue began to seem a bit wimpy, especially after *M*A*S*H* went off the air and *Oprah* cut into Phil's audience.

Were men becoming too much like women?

Rumors began to spread that sensitive men in North Dakota had started to lose interest in football and to experience trouble solving problems that involved long division. Theater owners in Chicago reported unprecedented numbers of men flocking to matinees of *Terms of Endearment*, sitting through several viewings and weeping audibly. Several guys in South Bend, Indiana, began displaying disturbing symptoms: they could no longer operate their chain saws, and they were having difficulty parallel parking. Shopkeepers in Seattle, Washington, reported sharp declines in the retail sales of 4 x 4 trucks, handguns, duct tape, and barbecue grills. Lawn care suffered throughout the Midwest. And woman everywhere reported that their men were losing interest in oral sex.

It was apparent to everyone that men had crossed the line. "We want our chauvinist pigs back!" declared the president of BOW WOW (Better Organization of Women Who Oppose Wimps). "Stop asking us how we feel, guys, just feel us up!"

To rejuvenate the macho man, BOW WOW hired Roberto Sly, a poet, lecturer, and former meat-packer, to root out feminine tendencies and rouse the wild-man side of the male population. Sly's agenda was to increase a man's pride in his manhood and end the wimp era. These were the humble roots of the now popular Iron John Wayne movement.

Sly's first act was to organize men-only retreats into the backwoods. At campsites across America, men stripped naked. They built huge ritualistic bonfires burning their Calvin Klein underwear, Ralph Lauren polo shirts, and Gap jeans. They were given tribal masks, wild-animal costumes, and military garb to wear. As the flames lit their joyful faces, these neo-Neanderthals played the conga drums and air guitars. Most often they sang and beat their drums to Frank Sinatra's "My Way."

Between sets, they watched macho movies like *Lethal Weapon, The Terminator,* and *Rambo,* shown on 35-mm projectors with really long extension cords. They read aloud from male action-adventure books. They staged fistfights and shouting matches. Stooped down on all fours, they pawed the ground, gurgled, bleated, and made wolf calls. Not only did they summon the wild man within, they scared off the wildlife without.

They called themselves New Age Masculinists, and they took a solemn oath to never eat yogurt, quiche, or sushi, even if they were starving to death in a shopping mall and the only oasis was a frozen yogurt stand.

They learned always to stand tall in a sea captain's pose and, while sitting, never to cross their legs.

As for dealing with women, Sly reminded the men that they were creatures of action. "Show your teeth. Show your anger. Show your manliness," Sly commanded. "Don't be a sap. If she disagrees with you, go for the jugular: tell her she's gaining weight."

Group discussions followed the instructions and rituals. No one was allowed to talk about emotions, anger, sensitivity, or childhood traumas. Instead, participants were encouraged to block their pain, ignore their feelings, and tell stories about their own sexual exploits. Exaggeration was encouraged and even rewarded with the envy of other men in attendance.

Following a snack of meat loaf and mashed potatoes, Roberto Sly stood and told the story of Iron John Wayne, which he said was a metaphor for all men. The convoluted and seemingly incomprehensible tale involved Iron John's efforts to reclaim the golden balls that led him through eight stages of male growth. By the time Sly had explained the third stage ("Moist Earth Masculinity"), most men were fast asleep. No matter. By then Roberto Sly had stemmed the tide of androgyny in America.

The sensitive man died a quick and painless death in the forest. Macho man emerged from the woods and returned to hearth and home demanding dinner on the table, football on the TV, and oral sex in bed.

Some women complain that the Iron John Wayne movement was the reason for the Persian Gulf War. Others are grateful they're no longer responsible for lawn maintenance and vehicle repair.

Sex Ruins Everything

My friend Carol says that every eligible man should have an expiration date stamped on his forehead, like a carton of milk. "That way you'd know just how long he's going to last before turning sour on you."

Unfortunately, love (and I hesitate to use the word) doesn't come with any directions or boundaries or instructions (and forget the idea of a warranty altogether). Past experience doesn't even help much either because, even though you keep making the same mistakes over and over again, you make them with different men, so they seem like different mistakes.

Larry the dentist is a case in point, or just a case, as the point may be. I thought he really liked me. I mean, really, really liked me. And I liked the way he liked me, so we went out a couple of times. He talked about my meeting his friends. He told me I was gorgeous. He said he liked talking to me; he was interested in my ideas. Once he said, "I'm nervous because I really want you to like me." I told him that, in general, I was skeptical about the possibility of having a relationship in my life. He said, in general, he was eternally optimistic.

I gave him my novel, and he said my writing reminded him of Kurt Vonnegut. Later, he quoted passages of my book to me.

We talked about his family, my family, friends, long-gone relationships, the recent past.

Secondhand confirmation arrived from the mutual friend who'd introduced us. She said: "He said you were perfect. He said he could get lost in your hair. He said he wanted to invite you to Vermont for the weekend."

He wrote me a poem: "I remember the days when I couldn't remember the sights smells sounds of you. But today, the calmness belies the spinning and twirling of emotions—a merry-go-round of love."

I was flattered. I was enchanted. I was charmed. He was in my thoughts. On the bus one afternoon, as I was musing about him, thoughts came into my head, but I kept them hidden in my heart and was afraid to write them down at first. When I did, I called it "Fusion":

> When I was six, my mother told me that if I had been born a boy, I would have been named Larry. Confusion. All those months I existed inside my mother and no one knew whether I was a Boy or Girl. So, I grew up with this boy named Larry as part of me, and to him I assigned all the masculine traits I didn't understand about myself: the aggression, the temper, the fierceness, my set chin, my hairy legs. At twelve I wrote stories about Boy and Girl twins. They solved mysteries. I never told anyone about Larry, he was just there. Then a Larry came into my life. And it was like meeting that Boy side of me. Fusion. At last.

I began to think that, maybe, some day, I could write down the prose poem and even show it to him. A long shot, of course, but once you let that nasty optimism in the door, all kinds of possibilities take over.

One night, after dinner, we were sitting in my apartment and he kissed me lightly, on the lips. It was a passing gesture. He continued talking. I leaned over and kissed him. At first, his mouth was opened too wide, a chasm. And then we found the meeting place between lips and teeth and tongues. He leaned toward me, and we drifted down into the couch. It felt like we were melting together, like fusion floating. Then we were on the floor. My back was against the couch, wedged between him and the leather cushioning. Slow motion, kissing, sinking. "I really wanted to kiss you," I said. Buttons came undone and silent zippers, too. Clothes half off, falling away. He went into the kitchen to get me a glass of water. I remember the ice-cold water in my mouth and the sight of him standing at my bedroom door, beckoning me with a crooked finger and a wrinkly smile.

I followed him to my bed. He undressed me. The rest was between us, intimacy and passion, the combination that checks in the throat and sometimes scalds the eyes with hot tears.

I told myself it had been mutual, but in my secret heart I suspected that it had been more for me than for him. He didn't stay the night.

Two days later, he called late at night. "You know, I want to be really honest with you. I don't have casual sex or get involved in casual relationships, so I don't think we should have sex again. Not that I'm not attracted to you, or anything, but I just don't see our relationship going in that direction...Of course, I still want to see you again. I'm kind of busy for the weekend, so why don't we have dinner next Tuesday night? I really want us to be friends."

I played with this conversation, over and over, in the next few days, wondering how I could turn it around so it didn't sound so much like I was getting dumped because I had had sex with him. I was confused: Larry wanted to keep seeing me but didn't want to have sex; most of the guys in my past wanted to continue having sex, they just didn't want to keep seeing me in order to do it.

I thought and thought. I analyzed. Actually, I obsessed.

What did he mean by casual sex? Did he mean sex without the possibility of commitment? Or did he define casual sex as sex with someone he didn't want to have sex with again? Or, even worse, did he relate to my friend's definition: "Casual sex is sex with someone you don't really like."

Had I misread him? The compliments, the attention, the enthusiasm, the poetry, the hand that brushed my thigh, the way I'd catch him staring at me. Each gesture like a door opening and now slammed shut. Mixed signals, then.

I felt bad. He didn't want to have sex with me again. And, all of a sudden, I very much wanted to have sex with him. And here's the question: Why would you want someone who doesn't want you?

This very familiar state: wanting someone mostly because I couldn't have him. I'd completely tossed aside the fact that I'd had genuine doubts about him. When we first met, I described my feelings about him to my friends like this: "Well, we have no future, but we could have a great present." After all, we were really different. He was too young, too conventional, and too conservative for me. He played golf, I went to the movies. He got up at the crack of dawn, I never went to sleep before 3 A.M. His philosophy of life was "Excess in moderation." Mine was "Fantasy over reality, any day."

So, if I knew all that, why was I feeling so bad? Well, of course, I told myself, it all had to do with my childhood and my mother and my sense of self-esteem and all those other buzzwords. Oh, please, I thought, don't let this turn into another one of life's lessons that I needed to learn. (I'm so tired of growing as a person.) I decided that I was causing myself to feel bad, and, therefore, I could also cause myself to feel better. So I began to look for reasons to feel positive.

For a while, I appreciated that he'd been so honest with me. After all, I told myself, there are lots of guys who never tell you what they're thinking or feeling and you only figure it out after you haven't heard from them in three or four months. But then this appreciation faded when I realized his honesty would have been a lot more helpful if he had expressed his doubts before we'd had sex.

Take away the honesty and what was left? I toyed with the scenario that he was backing off because he liked me so much that he was scared and, as soon as I proved to him that there was nothing to fear, he'd relent. While I still like this scenario better than any other I could possibly concoct, I admit it's full of holes. First off, if he really liked me, he'd probably want to have sex with me again. And, more to the point, who can convince anyone that love isn't a scary proposition?

I decided to focus on this problem: B.S. (Before Sex), I had invited him to a fancy-dress party for the following week. A.S. (After Sex), he called to make arrangements for the party. I hemmed and hawed, having a hard time saying what was in my heart, which was essentially this: "I'm really confused about what went down between us in such a short time, I don't think we should go to this party together, and I hope your dick falls off and you die a miserable death."

I stammered out the part about not going to the party but held back on the rest of the speech because, in my heart of hearts, I was hoping that he'd argue with me and talk me out of disinviting him to the party. (Then I wouldn't want him dead, or dickless, for that matter.) Not that I needed to worry. He didn't fulfill my fantasy. In fact, he relented rather easily,

expressing regret mainly because he was missing an opportunity to wear his expensive new tux.

I know (well, I suspect) that if I hadn't had sex with him, we
would've gone to the party and had a wonderful time. We
would've had, probably, several more dinners, lots of phone
conversations. Maybe I would've met his friends, maybe he
would've met some of mine. Maybe he would've written me
more poetry that scanned better. Then again, maybe this is me
going off on another fantasy. Because, inevitably, we would've
had sex and, I'm quite sure, A.S., the same problems.

Anyway, here's the major observation I discovered—and I'm
going to italicize it because I may have uncovered the major
difference between men and women: *I had doubts about him before
we had sex; he had doubts about me after we had sex.*

Translation: Sex eliminates a good many doubts for women.
Or, I should say, good sex compensates for having to wrestle
with a few doubts. And, undeniably, having a man inside you
changes you. This totally confuses men. I don't think they can
begin to understand how sex internalizes a woman's feelings,
fusing the physical with the emotional.

And, not understanding, men get confused. They withdraw.

So, sex ruins everything. After it makes you feel good, it
makes you feel sad and alone. It makes you cry. It makes you
possessive and mean and mad. It shatters your fantasies. It
clouds your judgment and destroys your reason. It makes you
lose control, and it scares you. It turns every minor incident
into a major experience. It makes everything seem lopsided. It
takes a nice evening and turns it into a potential battlefield. It
makes you long for feelings that aren't there. It makes you
crazy, and it breaks your heart. It's a lot like love, at least when
it's good. The only time sex doesn't feel bad is when it's not
good, and who wants sex that's not good, anyway?

When Larry called and I told him we shouldn't go to the party, I also said, "Sex ruins everything." He said if I wrote a book with that title, it would sell a million copies.

Instead I wrote this chapter, and curious about how Larry would react, I sent him a copy and then called and asked for his opinion. He said, "You've really captured what happened between us very accurately except for one glaring problem. I think you're confusing sex with love."

Of course I am. That's what women do, and what's more, we do not understand why men don't. If you could write a book explaining how men can separate love from sex, I want to tell him, you could sell ten million copies.

A Grim Fairy Tale

Anita in Wonderland

Anita was beginning to get very tired sitting alongside her college classmates on the lawn outside the library and having nothing to do. Once or twice she had peeped into the law books her friends were reading, but the books had no pictures or conversations in them. "And what is the use of a book," thought Anita, "without pictures or conversation?"

So she was considering in her own mind what was so fascinating about a case called *Row v. Wade* when a black rabbit ran close by her. There was nothing so remarkable in that; nor did Anita think it *very* much out of the way to hear the rabbit say to himself, "Oh dear! Oh dear! My secretary quits without giving notice. What shall I do?" (When she thought about it later, it occurred to her that she ought to have wondered at this, but at the time it seemed quite natural.) But when the Black Rabbit turned and offered Anita a job, she started to her feet, for it flashed across her mind that she had never even considered working for a rabbit, much less one who hadn't even mentioned profit sharing.

Burning with curiosity, Anita ran after the Black Rabbit and, just in time, saw him pop down a large rabbit hole on the corner of Mass Ave and K Street.

In another moment, down went Anita after him, never once considering how in the world she was to get out again or whether she had cab fare home.

She fell for a very long time and finally landed, with a thud, on a conference table at the bottom of the tunnel. On the table was a can of Coca-Cola, and tied around the can was a paper label with the words DRINK ME beautifully printed in large letters. Next to the soda was a videotape with a lot of XXXs stamped on the box, and tied around the tape was another paper with the words WATCH ME beautifully printed in large letters.

The Black Rabbit sat at the head of the table, and tied around his neck was another piece of paper with the words DATE ME beautifully printed in large letters.

"Curiouser and curiouser!" cried Anita. (She was so much surprised that for the moment she quite forgot how to speak good English.)

Just then, a little door opened, and into the room walked three odd-looking characters. The Black Rabbit introduced them as the Queen of Spades, the Duchess, and the Mad Hatter. "These are my law clerks," explained the Black Rabbit. "Let the marketing meeting begin."

"Who are you?" the Duchess asked Anita. "Explain yourself."

"I can't explain myself, I'm afraid," said Anita. "Because I'm not myself, you see."

"I don't see," said the Mad Hatter.

"Anita is my new assistant," proclaimed the Rabbit.

"Assistant? You promised me that job. I thought the new girl was your secretary," wailed the Mad Hatter.

"She's been promoted," explained the Black Rabbit. "So mind your own business."

"If everybody minded their own business," announced the Queen of Spades, "the world would go round a deal faster than it does."

The Duchess mumbled something about sucking up to the boss.

"Take some more Coca-Cola," the Black Rabbit said to Alice.

"I've had nothing yet," Alice replied in an offended tone, "so I can't take more."

"You mean you can't take *less*," said the Hatter. "It's very easy to take *more* than nothing."

Anita was quite confused and didn't know how to reply. After a brief but awkward pause, the Duchess leaned across the table and whispered, "Curtsy while you're thinking what to say. It saves time."

"Consider anything, only don't cry!" advised the Black Rabbit, who grinned and grinned and began to vanish quite slowly, beginning with the end of his tail and ending with the grin, which remained some time after the rest of him had gone.

"She made the boss disappear!" shouted the Mad Hatter.

"Off with her head!" yelled the Queen.

"Call Personnel!" screamed the Duchess.

Anita turned and ran through the little door, and she kept on running until she emerged from the tunnel at Delaware and M Street. She raced back to her friends at the law library. Everyone wanted to know where Anita had been. She wanted to tell them about her strange adventures with the Black Rabbit, but she didn't think anyone would believe her, so she kept the story to herself.

The years passed and Anita became a well-respected professor of veterinary law at a small university in the Midwest. Then one day a group of very important government men asked her to appear before them in a court of law and talk about her adventures with the Black Rabbit, who was being nominated for a seat at a great tea party. "Begin at the beginning...and go on till you come to the end; then stop," they said to Anita.

Reluctantly, Anita told them everything that had happened to her with the Black Rabbit. She remembered to consider everything but not to cry.

After Anita left the courtroom, the Mad Hatter, the Duchess, and the Queen of Spades testified, and everything they said contradicted Anita's story.

Then the Black Rabbit appeared before the court and categorically denied every word Anita had uttered.

In the end, just as Anita had predicted, no one believed her story.

"It's a poor sort of memory that only works backward," the government men concluded unanimously.

Poor Anita! She was called very bad names in the press. Many people criticized her for following the Black Rabbit in the first place. Some said she was heartless because she had not cried while telling her story in court. Others wondered why she had not told her story to her friends, or at least confided the details of her escapades to the Committee for Abused Adventurers and Office Workers.

Anita was very confused by the reaction to her testimony and remembered that her mother had once said to her. "Tut, tut, child, everything's got a moral if only you can find it."

Soon after her appearance before the court, Anita was besieged by many book publishers and filmmakers who wanted to buy the rights to her story. "It's as large as life and twice as natural," said one Hollywood producer.

Now Anita gives speaking engagements across the country and earns as much as ten thousand dollars a night, talking about everything except the Black Rabbit. She has stopped trying to find a moral to her story, because once you've been through the looking glass, it takes all the running you can do just to keep in the same place.

Sexual Harassment

Dating Tactic for the Nineties?

LS: Hello.

FBI: Yes, um, I'm calling for a, um, Miss…Linda Sunshine who resides at 347 Beekman Street in the East Village.

LS: Who's this?

FBI: Uh, Miss Sunshine, this is Agent X987 of the FBI. That's the Federal Bureau of Investigation located in Washington, D.C.

LS: I think I know where the FBI is located.

FBI: Very good. Now, Miss Sunshine, the reason we have contacted you is that we are investigating the confirmation of a Mr. Brian Carey to the Supreme Court of the United States and we're checking into his background, you know, just routine stuff…Wait a minute, Marv. Is the tape recorder working?

LS: You're recording this conversation?

FBI: No.

LS: But I thought I heard you say—

FBI: No, you didn't.

LS: Oh.

FBI: Now, first, Miss Sunshine, do you know Mr. Brian Carey who resides at 27 West 152nd Street? Tall, stocky, red beard, not balding?

LS: Yes, that's him.

FBI: And can you describe the nature of your relationship with him?

LS: No.

FBI: You won't?

LS: No, I would—but I can't. I mean, I've tried but it's…well, complicated.

FBI: Well, how do others—people close to you—describe your relationship with Mr. Carey?

LS: Well, let's see. My girlfriend says it's like Brian and I are friends with our pants off. My shrink, well, she, she says it's a compulsive blending of two perfectly matched neurotic obsessives. My ex-boyfriend says it's a tool to make him jealous. My best guy friend says Brian is the last unhealthy relationship I'm ever going to have. My doorman says I'm seeing too much of "that delivery person." And my mother says I never call her.

FBI: We've established that. Perhaps we should just move on. What I want to ask you is this: Is there any reason—in your personal experience with Mr. Carey—that would lead you to believe that he's not fit to serve on the Supreme Court?

LS: Well, one thing, I guess. He's not a lawyer.

FBI: He's not?

LS: No. He's an architect.

FBI: Are you sure?

LS: Yes. At least that's what he told me.

FBI: Okay, well, that explains that.

LS: Huh? What does that mean?

FBI: Nothing, um, nothing (*laughter*) really. Okay, um, any-
       thing else, about his character that would prevent him
       from serving on the court?

LS: He never went to law school.

FBI: Perhaps he once dated a lawyer?

LS: I wouldn't know. Listen, why would the President
       nominate Brian? It doesn't make too much sense to me.

FBI: Well, you're aware, Miss Sunshine, that the pool of
       potential candidates is running mighty low these
       days...so that may be the reason. Whatever, ours is not
       to question why. I mean, we are the FBI after all.

LS: True.

FBI: Okay, well, anything else you can tell us? About Brian's
       character, I mean?

LS: His character, um, you mean, like his personal views and
       all that?

FBI: Yes, precisely.

LS: Okay, let's see: He's an atheist, I think. He hates his
       mother. He thinks children shouldn't be seen or heard.
       He despises the Republicans, and I don't think he's too
       crazy about the Democrats either. He's pro abortion and,
       I guess, anti everything else. He hangs out in bars a lot.
       He's got a bad temper, and he can be pretty pigheaded
       on most issues. Sometimes he can go for weeks without
       calling me. I really hate that a lot, you know. He did
       some drugs when he was younger, and I think he's gotten
       lots of speeding tickets. He's kind of reckless, you know.

FBI: Well, none of that could keep him off the bench.

LS: He doesn't own a television.

FBI: Really? Why he must—Miss Sunshine, is Mr. Carey a
       Communist?

LS: Not to my knowledge.

FBI: Pity. So, let's continue—please try to be a little more specific—about his character. You know, like his sexual preferences. Can you tell us anything about that?

LS: Well, from my personal experience, I can tell you this: He's a very, very good kisser.

FBI: Yes, that has been confirmed from another source.

LS: Who?

FBI: I'm sorry, we never give out names.

LS: How about initials?

FBI: No.

LS: Well, the woman who told you this, is she pretty?

FBI: Gee, I don't know. She sounded nice on the phone. As my mother—a saint, really, my mother—used to say: Pretty is as pretty does.

LS: And she does, I'm sure. Tell me this: Does she live in Pennsylvania?

FBI: My mother?

LS: No, your source.

FBI: I can't reveal that. Now...uh, Marv, okay?...Right ... Uh, Miss Sunshine, please, can I get back to my questions?

LS: Okay...I guess.

FBI: Now, has Mr. Carey ever made reference to you about...You'll excuse me if you find this question offensive, but it has to be asked: Has he ever said anything about pubic hairs in his Coke?

LS: Agent X987, Brian Carey would never say anything like that! You don't know him! Brian Carey does not drink soda. I've never even seen him within ten feet of a Coke can.

FBI: Are you sure?

LS: Yes. I mean, the closest he's ever come to a comment like that was once, I think, once, he mentioned something about an eyelash in his Heineken.

FBI: An eyelash in his Heineken, eh? Marv, d'you hear that? Now we're getting some— Let me ask you this: Has Mr. Carey ever discussed pornographic movies with you?

LS: Again, Agent X987, you are barking up the wrong man. Brian Carey hates movies, all movies.

FBI: Then I guess he never mentioned a man named Long Dong Silver to you?

LS: No, but wait a minute, he once mentioned Barton Fink.

FBI: Barton Fink? Is he related to Long Dong Silver?

LS: I don't think so.

FBI: Well, we'll get some agents on it anyway. This next question is very important, so, please, think carefully before answering. To the best of your personal knowledge, has Mr. Carey ever violated Title VII of the Civil Rights Act?

LS: Title vee-eye-eye? You mean like segregation?

FBI: Miss Sunshine, really, Title VII concerns sexual harassment. And you call yourself a feminist! Ha! Let me rephrase the question. Has Mr. Carey, in any way, by his actions or words, given you cause to think he was sexually harassing you?

LS: Well, yes, actually, all the time. In fact, it's one of his most charming features. I mean, no one can sexually harass a woman quite like Brian Carey, and I'm not just talking about suggestive conversation in the workplace. That's child's play for a man like Brian. I mean, he's so good, he can sexually harass a woman on the phone, long-distance, while she's paying for the call. And what's more, he's personally harassed me, several times, through the mail—sometimes, concurrently, on the phone, in the mail, and in person in the same week. Let me tell you this, Agent X987, and I'd say this in a court of law— once you've been sexually harassed by Brian Carey, you stay harassed. He kind of spoils you for any other nominee to the Supreme Court, if you know what I mean.

FBI: Oh my, that's quite a recommendation. Do you think he'd go out with me?

LS: An FBI agent? Gee, I don't know how to answer that question.

FBI: Oh, never mind then. Listen, just a few more questions. We have an unconfirmed report from a reliable source, that Mr. Carey had his cat—Marv, what was the cat's name? Oh, yeah—Anyway, that Mr. Carey had his cat, Bob, killed and then frozen. Can you confirm that accusation?

LS: Well, you know, Bob was really, really ill and he was very old.

FBI: Please just answer yes or no. Did Mr. Carey kill the cat?

LS: Listen, that was a very painful time in his life, Brian was under a lot of stress—

FBI: Yes or no, Miss Sunshine.

LS: Okay, yes.

FBI: Aw-right! Marv, we got 'em on the cat. Thank you for your cooperation, Miss Sunshine. You've done a great service for the FBI and for the country...

LS: Listen, you know, Bob was getting IV, he couldn't eat; I mean, he was twenty-three years old, the poor thing could barely stand on his—

FBI: That's fine, Miss Sunshine, we'll call you again if we need any further information.

LS: But Bob's...about Bob, I mean, if you'd heard his pathetic—

FBI: Good-bye Miss Sunshine. We'll send you a transcript of this conversation.

LS: But you said you weren't recording it.

FBI: Yeah, right. My advice to you is get a lawyer and find something nice to wear on television. You may be called to testify.

LS: Testify?

FBI: Yes, just in care the hearing goes before the Senate. You're not squeamish about appearing in front of TV cameras?

LS: Oh, no, I've trained with Dorothy Sarnoff. You know, for my book-promotion tours. She told me I had nice hair— for television.

FBI: Yes, we know that.

LS: You do?

FBI: Miss Sunshine, we're the FBI, remember?

LS: Oh, right.

FBI: You can hang up now.

LS: No, that's fine, you hang up first.

FBI: No, you.

LS: Listen, it's kind of late for this kind of conversation. I mean, it must be after one in the morning.

FBI: Yeah, I know and I'm starving. You probably wouldn't be interested 'cause it's so late and all, but, you know, I'm not far from your house...

LS: Yeah? I thought you were calling from Washington.

FBI: No, actually I'm calling from the phone booth across the street from your apartment.

LS: Really? You mean, if I look out my window—

FBI: Yeah, that's me. See? I'm waving to you, and, hey!, is that your light flashing up there?

LS: Yup.

FBI: Well, what do you—Listen, you know that little bar

called the Lion's Head? Well, of course, I know you do,
you've been there, by our count, forty-eight times in the
past six months.

LS: That sounds right.

FBI: So maybe I could persuade you to come out. Hey, Marv,
cut the tape record—

The Clarence Thomas Lexicon

No matter how many opinions Clarence Thomas eventually writes while on the Supreme Court, he will be remembered as the man who brought Long Dong Silver into congressional records.

Because of his influence, office politics have changed. Men are confused. They want to know: What constitutes sexual harassment?

The answer is simple: Almost everything can be construed as sexual harassment depending upon the way it is said.

One general rule of thumb is to think of your female co-workers as you would your sister. Yes, she is a woman. No, she is not a sexual object. Yes, your parents probably like her more than they like you.

In more concrete terms, here are some specific guidelines:

1. No jokes about Ted Kennedy, Willie Smith, Mike Tyson, or Richard Gere.

2. No teasing, attacking, razzing, or ribbing. Will women take this kind of talk personally? You bet they will.

3. No winking. (Exceptions can be made only if you are holding a marketing meeting on a dusty train track.)

4. No terms of endearment. Use only the words honey and sugar when you are referring to tea or coffee.

5. No obscenities or innuendos. Stick to single entendres.

6. Do not lick your lips in front of a female co-worker unless you are both eating spareribs.

7. Do not stare at any part of a woman's anatomy, with one possible exception: you may stare at her feet if you are offering a heartfelt apology.

8. No porn magazines (whole or cut up) or X-rated videos in the office—not even for the sake of art.

9. No touching, no kissing. Tongues should not be seen or heard.

10. No anatomical references in front of female co-workers unless you are a certified medical practitioner.

Specific Words and Phrases Men Can No Longer Say to Women

Seen any good movies?

My wife is out of town for the weekend.

How about dinner?

How much does this job mean to you?

Did you hear the one about the traveling videocassette salesman?

What's that floating in your iced tea?

You look very pretty today.

Didn't I see you in last month's issue of *Penthouse?*

Had any lately?

You're overreacting.

I thought women liked that kind of thing.

The Successfully Dysfunctional Family

All happy families resemble one another, but each dysfunctional family is dysfunctional in its own way.
—Leo Tolstoy,
Anna!
(the made-for-television screenplay
adapted from his novel)

Dysfunctional families come in all shapes and sizes. Mine was a size 38 extra long, with a little extra room sewn into the seat.

My childhood was greatly affected by the fact that I was born long before the invention of quality time. Back then, mothers and fathers spent huge quantities of time with their offspring. Call it ignorance. "Who knew about this quality-time business?" my mother will often ask. "In our day, quality time meant you had food in the refrigerator, the rent was paid for the next month, and no one at the dinner table was getting sued or recovering from surgery."

My parents are not the only people who are confused by the concept of quality time. Many books have been written on the subject in the hopes of explaining to modern parents the damage they can inflict on their children by not allocating time into quality increments. "Raw time is like nonhomogenized milk," explains one child psychologist. "It can make both you and your child sick to your respective stomachs. We now recognize that every moment spent with your child should be as jam-packed with learning, fun, and bonding as humanly possible for psychological health. The proof is in the pudding. Parents didn't begin doling out quality time until the mid-1980s, which explains why so many Baby Boomers are currently in therapy or on medication."

We are the dysfunctional generation, and celebrity dysfunctional families have become the most popular guests on the talk-show circuit, the subjects of bestselling books, and the topics of discussion in anonymous meetings across the country. Everyone, in short, is jumping on the neo-neurotic bandwagon.

I don't mean to brag, but I take great pride in reporting that members of my family have been in the otherly abled psychological forefront for many decades. We were a dysfunctional group long before the term was ever used on national television. For this reason, my grandmother can barely contain herself when she watches *Donahue* or *Oprah*.

"These know-it-alls act like they've invented emotional abuse and addictive behavior," she'll often rant and rage at the television set when I visit her in Miami Beach. "Whole generations of this family were dysfunctional way before television was even invented. Why, you had a great-grandfather, he should rest in peace, who was known throughout Schönhausen as the village alcoholic. Drank like a fish. And my aunt Mavis, your great-great-aunt, was married to a Cossack who beat her senseless once a month. Mavis didn't have low self-esteem, she had *no* self-esteem to have married that moron in the first place.

"And you want to talk nervous breakdowns? We've had relatives in every major world war and foreign conflict who were kept out of service because of a loose screw. None of our men have ever seen combat.

"We've had manic depressives, attempted suicides, and even one bona fide psychotic. Leonard. True, Leonard was a cousin by marriage of your Uncle Morris, but still, we always considered him family. There he sat at every Seder with his automatic rifle; it scared the living daylights out of Great-Grandma Nettie, who was from the Old Country and didn't know from such technology. Nettie made Leonard leave the gun on the seat for Elijah, wrapped in plastic, naturally, because it was so greasy."

If you don't stop Grandma by this point, she gets out the photographs. "Just look in our family album—you'll find weepers, dreamers, nail biters, hysterics, bed wetters, screamers, hypochrondriacs, neurotics, womanizers, check bouncers. We got 'em all. Ach! It gives me a pain in my gall bladder when I think about the fortune we could've made if talk shows had been around in my day."

Family pride runs deep in my family; it courses through our blood like my brother-in-law's Corvette on the Garden State Parkway. We have often discussed having a family crest made. It would be shaped like a poker table and contain symbols of the three most prominent genetic trademarks of the family clan: obesity, kleptomania, and agoraphobia.

Parent-child relationships are as troubled in my family as anything you'll see on daytime talk shows. I have several cousins who've moved clear across the continent just to get away from their parents and others who still live at home well

into their thirties and forties. Separation anxiety is endemic in
our family, and even our family pets tend to hyperventilate
during family gatherings.

We gamble, smoke, and lie a lot, especially among ourselves. We spend our time together insulting each other and
our time apart being critical of our weaker members.

Most of my blood relatives are in complete denial. We think
of ourselves as a happy, close, and fun-loving family, yet every
one of us has frequent stomachaches and migraine headaches.
We cry easily and often, especially when Grandpa Max joins
us for dinner.

Unfortunately, we are given little credit in the media.
Despite the thousands of dollars we've spent collectively on
psychiatric help, none of us has ever been written up in any
scientific journal. Even more disturbing is the lack of attention
from the media.

My grandmother would love to share the spotlight with
celebrity dysfunctional families such as the Ronald Reagans,
the Bing Crosbys, the Joan Crawfords, the Kennedys, and the
Windsors of England. She feels that too much hoopla is made
over celebrity child-abusers while the ordinary citizens who
neglect their children or cause violence to their household pets
are never noticed by the press.

"It's very unfair," agrees the publisher of a prominent New
York newspaper, "but the public is more interested in the
dysfunctions of the rich and famous than in those of Mr. and
Mrs. America."

But the public should not be fooled by the headlines. There
are successful dysfunctional families in all walks of life. You
don't have to be a movie star, president of a country, or the
future king of England to live in a dysfunctional family. Your

family is just as important and probably as dysfunctional as any other.

"Always remember that blood is thicker than water," says my Aunt Elsie, the overweight kleptomaniac who hasn't left her house in three years, so she's forced to steal from family. It's not as bad as it sounds. When we have Passover dinner with Aunt Elsie and Uncle Abe, we leave our wallets in the car.

Take This Test

Are You Prejudiced Against Single People?

A recent Galloping Poll noted an 87 percent rise in prejudice against single people. Reported one pollster, "This is the age of family values and safe sex, so single people represent a real threat to the status quo." Other surveys have confirmed that single people are considered more frivolous and less reliable than their married counterparts. Even though single people pay higher taxes, they have a harder time obtaining mortgages from banks and short-term handouts from friends and co-workers.

As an ever growing minority, single people are generally ignored by politicians and snubbed at their high-school reunions. They suffer more criticism from their parents and siblings. Forced to live in a world of secrecy and pretense, single people spend lonely nights in front of the television set in lieu of appearing in public without an escort for the evening.

Single people have always been treated like second-class citizens, pitied by their married friends and ridiculed by the media, especially those of the cultural elite who write and produce sitcoms for television. Single women on television are either dim-witted or bad-tempered; single men are vain, arrogant, or mentally retarded.

Prejudice against single people is marked by the growth of groups of married supremacists now waging war against single people in this country. The most recent incident was the riot in Dude County that started when Ronnie Kingston, a recently divorced woman, turned down a date with an eligible dentist on *The New Dating-for-Dollars Game Show*. On national television, Ronnie said, "No, thank you, doctor. I'm not really interested in dating at this point in my life." The dentist was so outraged that he filed a lawsuit against Ronnie for "cruel and unusual embarrassment in prime time."

During the trial, the videotape of Ronnie's rejection was shown repeatedly on televison, and the incident was debated on every talk show in America. Ronnie's mother appeared on *Donahue* and, with tears in her eyes, pleaded with mothers of eligible dentists to forgive her wayward daughter. "I don't know what we did wrong with Ronnie. She was a rebel from the day she was born." The distraught woman wept on Donahue's shoulder. "Believe me, her sister Rachel never would have done such a thing. Rachel's married to a pharmacist. They live in a very nice part of New Jersey. Look at these pictures of my grandchildren, Phil."

Sympathy for the rejected dentist continued to mount, especially after his trial testimony was broadcast live on television. Though his face was obliterated by a big blue circle, his pleas for financial retribution were heard loud and clear. "I was rejected on national television," bemoaned the big blue circle. "If Ronnie wasn't interested in dating during this period of her life, then why was she a contestant on the dating show? What kind of racket is this? What's happening to single women today?"

Many people felt that the logic of the dentist's argument was irrefutable, which is probably why, in hindsight, people were so infuriated when the Dude County jury returned a verdict of not guilty and Ronnie walked away from the trial without having to pay a dime. Only moments after the verdict was announced, a riot broke out in the streets. Married supremacists smashed the windows of health clubs, florist shops, lingerie stores, salad bars, and computer-dating companies across the city. They held a massive bonfire in the town square, burning hundreds of confiscated Filofaxes. The streets were strewn with shredded personal ads.

In the wake of the rioting, many civic leaders joined together to help defuse the emotional outburst against the unwed. The American Association for the Advancement of Single People, AAASP, called for a peaceful march on singles bars across the nation, and more than two million people turned out to protest and mingle. The Reverend Jessica Jackman organized a Rainbow Coalition luncheon between single people and married couples. "When will married couples finally acknowledge that everyone starts life as a single person?" Jackman asked the crowd that gathered at TGIF in New York City. "Single people are more than just your baby-sitters and delivery boys; they are the future married people of America."

Many experts feel that prejudice against single people stems from ignorance. Aside from what you hear from stand-up comics, how much do you really know about the life of a single person in today's society? To find out, the AAASP recommends that you take the following test, developed by a group of researchers at Dartmouth's Singles Only Data Research Laboratory and Laundromat. The test is meant to help social workers determine the level of prejudice against single people in the average person. Answer the following questions as honestly as you can.

1. All single people
   a) are great dancers
   b) want to be married
   c) just pretend to be happy in order to annoy their married friends and family

2. Do you consider being single
   a) a sign of independence
   b) an opportunity for experimentation and exploration
   c) punishment for not being married

3. Every single woman should be married
   a) before giving birth
   b) before reaching menopause
   c) at least once in her life

4. Every single man should be married
   a) to a woman his mother likes
   b) to the mother of his children
   c) to a woman his own age

5. Do you think single people are
   a) happier than married people
   b) jealous of married people
   c) a threat to family values and the American way of life

6. In comparison to married people, do you think single people are
   a) more lonely
   b) less lonely
   c) better dressed

7. With more disposable income, single people are more
   likely to
   a) vacation frequently
   b) support their parents
   c) pay for psychotherapy

8. The best part about being single is
   a) Club Med
   b) the sex
   c) no one tells you what to wear

9. The worst part about being single is
   a) Club Med
   b) the sex
   c) no one tells you what to wear

10. Single people excel at
    a) racquetball
    b) *Jeopardy*
    c) avoiding family gatherings

SCORING:
   If you are married: you are not supposed to score.
   If you are single: you should know by now whether or not
you've scored.

Silicone Breast Implants

Medical Miracle or Automotive Wonder?

Despite the current controversy between members of the medical establishment, the federal government, the feminist movement, and flat-chested women of all ages, races, and bra sizes, breast augmentation is still one of the most popular plastic surgery procedures in this country. In January 1992, *People* magazine reported that "over two million women have received silicone implants since they've been on the market, and more than 89,000 in 1990 alone." It has subsequently been learned that this figure was inadvertently inflated.

As reported on *The Jenny Jones Show*, the actual number of women who have received silicone breast implants is just slightly over one million. The two million figure calculated the number of implants (obviously two per woman—although a transsexual in Baton Rouge reportedly implanted three breasts into his rather expansive chest) as opposed to the actual number of breast implant *recipients*. As the Surgeon General recently commented: "Leave it to some bozo medical statistician (probably a lonely man) to count breasts, not women."

Even so, one million women and two million new breasts

(or, two million and one if you want to be truly accurate) is a fairly impressive statistic in its own right. In the past, only the rich and famous could afford the luxury of purchasing a new chassis, but times (and health-care benefits) have clearly changed. Plastic surgery is now an equal-opportunity procedure, and for the past decade women have been flocking to their doctors in the hopes of transforming themselves from a Twiggy to a Dolly Parton.

Today, a woman is no longer complimented by such uninspired expressions as "Gee, you look pretty tonight!" Now, a woman on a good day is more likely to be asked the ultimate nineties complimentary question: "Can I get the name of your surgeon?"

Why are we so obsessed with plastic surgery? Psychologists tell us that the desire for a perfect body begins early in a young girl's life. Dr. Margaret Banning, chief pediatrician at the Corning Research Clinic in Elvira, New York, conducted a three-year survey of more than two thousand girls between the ages of eight and fourteen, polling their views on self-confidence, personal preferences, role models, and mall activities. The participants were asked to list, in order of importance, the things they consider most crucial to their personal well-being. Ninety-five percent of these girls included on their list: big hair, nonfat frozen yogurt, a good education, a warm puppy, driving lessons, a date with Luke Perry, big bosoms, thick lips, and thin thighs.

"We give Barbie dolls to our daughters and then wonder why they're obsessed with perfect bodies," Dr. Banning observed at a recent workshop for working mothers and toy manufacturers. "One little girl in Topeka told me that if she didn't look like Madonna by the time she turned thirteen, she was going to ask Santa for breast augmentation."

The little girl in Topeka is not the only child who wants to look like Madonna. (Although some of the girls in the racially balanced Corning survey expressed a desire to look like Paula Abdul or La Toya Jackson.) It is difficult to calculate the influence that movie and rock stars have had in promoting plastic surgery.

The first acknowledged star to admit to some form of anatomical reconstruction was Fanny Brice, the beloved Ziegfeld comedienne who was later portrayed by Barbra Streisand in *Funny Girl*. In 1923, Brice told reporters that her nose was not only redone, it was "condemned and torn down." Since then, Brice's openness has been equaled, if not surpassed, by other show business personalities. Some stars flaunt their new bodies (Cher, Melanie Griffith, Joan Rivers, Michael Jackson), others refused to admit or deny (Jane Fonda, Sally Field, Michelle Pfeiffer, Jessica Rabbit). Sylvester Stallone admitted that he has no problem with plastic surgery. "Why not do it?" he told a reporter. "You have bodywork done on your car."

Stallone's analogy is not without precedent. After all, silicone is a substance that is more likely to be found in an automotive repair shop than in the human body.

For anyone contemplating the injection of silicone into his or her most private parts, it might be interesting to answer the question: What exactly is silicone? Well, briefly, silicone is defined by *Webster's* as "any of various polymeric organic silicon compounds obtained as oils, greases, or plastics." It is used for water-resistant and heat-resistant lubricants, varnishes, binders, and electric insulators. Silicone is popular for caulking windows, lubricating automobile transmissions, increasing bust lines, and reducing facial wrinkles.

Not surprisingly, California has the highest per capita rate of plastic surgery and transmission failure. In Santa Cruz, an enterprising plastic surgeon, Dr. Frederick Wakabushi, and his son, Freddy Junior, a licensed mechanic, have taken advantage of the multipurpose quality of silicone by opening a chain of stores called Father and Son: Boobs and Lubes. The stores offer auto and bust repair in one quick, convenient location. Patrons can have a tummy tuck from dad while junior rotates the tires. Prices are rock bottom. "We buy industrial-grade silicone in bulk and pass the savings along to our customers," says Dr. Wakabushi.

The first Lubes and Boobs shop opened in 1990 in the Alameda shopping mall and was such a success that two other mall outlets opened the next year, in Woodland Hills and East Los Angeles. All three locations were doing quite well until Lubes and Boobs was sued by a disgruntled customer named Myra Worthinheim, a manicurist from Burbank. In testimony given before the Los Angeles Better Business Bureau, Ms. Worthinheim claimed that Freddy Junior liposuctioned the rear end of her hatchback while Dr. Wakabushi realigned her spinal column. Ms. Worthinheim claimed that as a consequence of her association with Lubes and Boobs, she now walks on her hands and eats with her feet.

"And my hatchback hasn't been the same since I drove out of the Alameda mall," Ms. Worthinheim added. "My trunk space is so tight that I can barely fit a bag of groceries behind the driver's seat."

Ms. Worthinheim is suing Dr. Wakabushi for mental cruelty and a new set of whitewalls.

In his defense, Dr. Wakabushi offered to settle out of court. "It was a simple misunderstanding—human error," he claimed in his deposition. "We were having a busy day, and my son mixed up the paperwork."

Ms. Worthinheim's story should serve as a warning to all women who are considering reconstructive surgery. The federal government is now conducting studies to evaluate the safety of silicone implants, although most doctors agree that injecting silicone (or any other varnish, plastic compound, or heat sealant) into your body may be hazardous to your health.

The AMA has advised that silicone from breast implants can leak into your lymph nodes and other vital organs. The leakage from silicone implants can cause connective-tissue diseases such as rheumatoid arthritis and can lead to a sometimes deadly buildup of fibrous tissue in the lungs. Silicone can thicken, making your implants harden and causing loss of sensation in the healthy breast tissue.

Silicone is also hazardous when used to alleviate wrinkles in the face. During this procedure, the surgeon uses a fine needle to inject droplets of silicone beneath the skin. Once injected into the tissue, however, silicone becomes part of the lattice-work of fibrous tissue and can be removed only by taking away the tissue in which it's embedded. You may therefore remove your wrinkles but, ultimately, a good part of your face may go along with them.

Finally, the AAA warns that silicone injections can severely impair the miles per gallon you are now getting from premium gasoline.

Health Risks for Single People

A very important but little noticed article on health risks to single people was recently published in the *New Jersey Journal of Medicine*. The authors, Dr. Janine Jamawitz, who holds the Kathryn Gibbs Chair at Brigham and Women's Hospital in Boston, and her colleagues from other leading medical centers in New Jersey, reviewed nearly two thousand studies, polls, magazine surveys, and job applications to evaluate the physical and emotional health of single people. Their study shows that single people have very different health problems than married people. Their findings can help focus attention on the factors which can most significantly increase the lifespan and decrease the anxiety level of the single person.

1. *Smoking.* Statistics confirm that single people are twenty times more likely to smoke than married people since they do not have a spouse who constantly complains about dirty ashtrays and foul-smelling breath. Single people are also at higher risk of suffering the effects of secondary smoke since they are more likely to hang out in nightclubs and vacation in Europe, where smoking is still socially acceptable.

The Surgeon General advises that quitting smoking will greatly enhance the possibility of avoiding heart and lung disease, although abstention from smoking can result in a decreased appreciation for spending long afternoons and late evenings in neighborhoods bars. Withdrawal from smoking illegal substances can induce a lowered appreciation of heavy metal music, nonsensical punch lines, and sugary foods. Many former hippies believe that the psychological trauma of such side effects totally offset any possible health advantages.

2. *Maintaining "ideal" weight.* Major fluctuations in weight gain and loss are detrimental to your health and embarrassing to explain to your friends and family. Still, most women cannot get off of the dieting-gaining seesaw. The problem is especially prevalent among single women, who tend to gain weight when they are in a comfortable relationship and lose weight if they are abandoned by their loved one. (The next highest risk group consists of married women who suspect their husbands of having an affair.)

The problem is exacerbated by the way most women feel about their bodies. In a recent survey, 43 percent of all married women said they were trying to lose weight, compared to 98 percent of single women.

"It's important to maintain your ideal weight while dating," explains one single woman who works part-time as a Weight Watchers consultant. "Otherwise you run the risk of blaming your thighs when you don't have a date on Saturday night."

Contrary to this statement, it has been proven that heavy thighs represent only a 25 percent risk factor in attracting a date. By far the more serious detriments include small breasts and the tendency to drool while sleeping on the beach or as a passenger in a moving vehicle.

3. *Stress.* Stress can cause a multitude of health problems ranging from heart palpitations, excessive sweating, backaches, and headaches to excessive nailbiting and repeated incidents of stubbed toes. Single women actually experience less stress than married people since they have more disposable income, no in-

laws, and no competition from wives of their husband's golf partners and coworkers. Single mothers, however, experience more stress than married mothers in terms of discussing anatomy-related topics with their sons. Single women without children experience the least number of stress-related problems except for incidents involving vacations, waiting in restaurants, and tipping during the holiday seasons.

4. *Physical activity.* Before the invention of the answering machine, single women faced the hazard of becoming sedentary while waiting for the telephone to ring. Today's modern technology has all but eliminated this risk factor. However, technology has also created a new condition called S.P.A. (Single Person's Angst). S.P.A. becomes evident after a single woman takes inventory of her living environment, noting the four or five phone extensions, two different telephone numbers, call waiting, a cellular phone, a mobile car phone, a fax machine, and an answering machine. Suddenly, the single woman realizes that despite the thousands of dollars spent for the most modern equipment, still, no one ever calls. The insight has caused severe trauma for many S.P.A. victims.

5. *High Cholesterol and hypertension.* Single people tend to ignore the health risks of these two conditions since both sound like diseases of married people. Most single people concentrate on diseases that sound like they belong to the unmarried: melancholia, tendinitis, post-traumatic shock syndrome, and stage fright.

6. *Nausea.* Studies have shown that single people experience a higher incidence of nausea than married people. In females, doctors explain this as a psychosomatic identification with pregnant woman. For men, nausea represents a recurring fear of commitment that is so strong it makes a guy want to puke. There is no known cure for the condition at the present time.

7. *Anxiety.* Single people face the constant threat of anxiety

attacks, especially if they live within a hundred fifty miles of their parents. Many patients suffering from anxiety take prescription drugs without their doctor's consent or knowledge. Other patients self-prescribe massive infusions of Häagen-Dazs and frequent visits to their local movie theater or video-rental store, even though neither of these regimens has been proven to be scientifically effective in the relief or cure of anxiety.

8. *Cuts, scrapes and minor abrasions.* Single women are more likely than married women to suffer from nicks and cuts, especially on their legs and underarms. Researchers are unable at this time to understand the reason for this phenomenon, although, through funding from a generous government grant, an extensive five-year investigation into the problem is currently being conducted at Duke University. Also included in the study is research into why twice as many single women as married complain of red rashes in the so-called bikini area of their anatomy. Scientists believe the epidermal condition is linked to a process called "waxing," a tribal ritual practiced mainly by single professional women. Doctors are anxious to understand the motives for this procedure, hoping it will also help explain a single woman's propensity for electrolysis, high-impact-aerobics, and shoes that are a size too small.

"We are trying to determine whether single women have a higher tolerance for pain than married women," explains Dr. Jamawitz. "Or are they simply more masochistic?" Results of the study are expected to be published before the turn of the century.

9. *Codependency.* While married people run a higher risk of becoming codependent on their spouses, single people often become codependent on people with whom they may have only a casual acquaintance, on co-workers or, in most extreme cases, on television personalities or movie stars. This is why

middle-aged women think they look like Michelle Pfeiffer when they wear black Spandex or why young men spend thousands of hours trying to develop Sylvester Stallone muscles. Dr. Jamawitz, an expert on the disease, has recently published a paperback book entitled *Codependency: When You Don't Have a Lifestyle of Your Own*. The book advises single people to turn off their television sets. "Get a life, for gosh sake," declares Dr. Jamawitz.

10. *Sexual addiction*. For single people, sexual addiction can be both frustrating and frightening. Today, life-threatening diseases have taken all the fun out of being sexually active. But still, some people are addicted to having sex and find that quitting is as difficult as dieting during the Christmas holidays. For this reason, many therapists have been developing regimens and techniques for breaking the curse of sexual addiction.

The most recent new technique is the Private Parts Patch. The P.P. Patch covers the erogenous areas most addicted to sexual gratification and can be individually adjusted according to personal preference. Some sexual addicts use the P.P. Patch only in the region of their genitals. Others cover their eyes, mouth, nose, neck, behind the ear, in the crook of their arm, or behind the knee. The fetish P.P. Patch comes in the shape of a woman's pump (size 7AAA).

A Grim Fairy Tale, Hotel, and Casino

Ivanarella

Once upon a time, a widowed gentleman lived in a fine house in Eastern Europe with his only daughter, Ivanarella. To provide his teenage girl with a mother's care, the man married a woman with two young daughters who, he hoped, would be playmates for Ivanarella and teach her how to speak English with a thick accent.

Sad to say, the man died soon afterwards and the girl's stepmother, who was harsh and mean, turned their fine house into a ski resort and forced Ivanarella to run the gift shop all by herself. Poor Ivanarella spent her days folding sweaters and trying to unload a shipment of puce ski goggles while her stepsisters flirted with the cute ski instructors.

One day, a rich and powerful American, known throughout Eastern Europe as the Prince of Floral Park, visited the lodge to practice his stem christies and find himself a wife. He said he would marry the first woman who could ski Suicide Run with him. Every eligible maiden in the village grabbed her skis and raced to the top of mountain. Ivanarella wanted to join them, but her wicked stepmother made her stay at the lodge and prepare the hot cocoa. Standing over a hot hot plate, Ivanarella wept bitter tears into the Nestlé's hot chocolate mix.

But at that moment, out of a cloud of magic powdered sugar, appeared a round-faced little man in a hooded cloak. "Dry those tears," said the little man. "You can't go skiing like that, your face will freeze."

Ivanarella stopped crying. "Who are you?"

"I'm your fairy godperson. I'm here to make the cocoa so you can go ski with the Prince of Floral Park."

"But I don't have any skis," wailed Ivanarella.

With a wave of a magic wand, a pair of Rossignols magically appeared on Ivanarella's feet.

As Ivanarella grabbed the T-bar, her fairy godperson commanded her, above all things, not to stay on the slopes past sunset and, if she got lucky, to practice safe sex.

The Prince noticed Ivanarella the moment she slid off the T-bar. "Who is that girl in purple?" he asked the team of lawyers who followed him everywhere. No one knew. Not even her wicked stepmother or nasty stepsiblings recognized Ivanarella in her skin-tight purple ski outfit and matching ski mask.

The Prince asked Ivanarella for the next run, and down the mountain they soared. When the Prince began to lose his balance, Ivanarella yelled, "Get into your snow plow!," and following her advice, he made it to the bottom of the mountain without so much as a tumble. The Prince leaned over to kiss Ivanarella, but before she could remove her ski mask, the sun began to set beyond the hill. Ivanarella turned and ran away, but in her haste, she lost one of her ski boots. The Prince grabbed the boot and said he would marry the first woman whose foot fit into it.

The news of the Prince's announcement caused a minor stampede of single women from across the White Carpathian

Mountains. Each one tried on the boot, but it didn't fit any of them.

The Prince was about to give up the search when one of his lawyers visited the gift shop to buy a Basket of Jams from Around the World for his wife back home in the States. The lawyer spotted poor Ivanarella crying in the storage room. (Her wicked stepmother had locked Ivanarella there that morning.) The lawyer took the key off the hook, unlocked the door, and asked Ivanarella to try on the ski boot. When it fit perfectly, he handed her a prenuptial agreement and called the Prince.

The Prince and Ivanarella were married and, the next day, flew to America to set up house in the Prince's castle on Fifth Avenue in New York City. Because of her working experience in the gift shop at home, Ivanarella was able to help the Prince run his auxiliary castles in Atlantic City and Palm Beach.

The couple lived a storybook kind of life until the day Ivanarella discovered that the Prince was skiing in Aspen with a Georgia peach. Soon Ivanarella was in divorce court, where she sued the Prince for committing adultery with fresh produce. Ivanarella and her lawyers haggled out an agreement with the Prince's lawyers, and finally, the judge awarded her millions and millions of dollars. Ivanarella took the money and bought herself a new body, a reconstructed face, a flattering new hairdo, and lots of positive P.R. from all her friends who wrote gossip columns. She appeared on the covers of *Vogue, Vanity Fair,* and *Lear's.* Soon she was endorsing a line of Ivanarella creams, body products, and perfume; a collection of blouses and leggings; and her first novel, *For Love of Alimony.*

Ivanarella's life story should serve as a lesson to all women. This is an urban fable with three morals:

1. A woman can be married, the mother of several healthy

children, have a great career, a swell figure, wardrobe, nannies, maids, homes, limos, and millions of dollars—and still find herself back in the singles market one day.

2. Just because a woman signs a few prenuptial agreements (Ivanarella signed four!), she need not feel obligated to stick to them. In summer camp, this is called a "Do-over", as in "I couldn't see the ball because the sun was in my eyes. It's a Do-over." Do-overs are useful in divorces, too.

3. It is just as easy to fall in love with a billionaire as it is with any rich guy. And more profitable too!

Yes, But Can Warren Beatty Breast-feed?

Forget the image of Clark Gable sweeping Vivian Leigh off her feet and up the red-carpeted staircase, or James Cagney smashing a grapefruit into Mae Murray's face, or Humphrey Bogart tossing Mary Astor to the cops. The virile Hollywood man now asserts his manhood by taking charge of the two A.M. feeding and wearing a Snugli in public.

Look at the images now appearing in our most popular magazines: Jack Nicholson juggling babies, Kevin Costner pushing a stroller, Mel Gibson swinging a toddler on the beach, William Hurt being sued for child support. Even the rock world has been rocked: The Boss recently became a father and Mick Jagger is a grandfather!

More and more Hollywood leading men are celebrating their fatherhood in print and on television. They arrive on late-night talk shows to plug their latest movies and discuss the politics of pacifiers or the problem of finding a good preschool. Where comedians like Bill Cosby used to mock the birthing process, now retelling birthing stories brings tears to the eyes of clowns like Howie Mandel or Robin Williams.

Today's most celebrated new poppa, Warren Beatty, recently

discussed witnessing the birth of his daughter with David
Frost, claiming it was "the biggest experience I've ever had," a
pretty impressive declaration given Warren's reputation with
females in the past. Warren joyfully added that his daughter
"recognized my voice the first second because she was used to
the voice in the womb...It was a great matter of pride to me
that she knew my voice as soon as she entered the world." One
has to wonder how many times the fetus was exposed to
Shampoo, Reds, Heaven Can Wait, Ishtar, and *Bugsy.*

Statistics give credence to the emerging role of fathers.
According to a Lee Strasberg survey made in 1974, only 27
percent of all movie-star fathers were present in the delivery
room when their children were born. Ten years later, the
number rose to 80 percent, and today it can be as high as 90
percent—and that's not even including bit players, stuntmen,
or extras.

Because of the popularity of fatherhood among the major
leading men in Hollywood, the pregnancy rate has soared in
Los Angeles County. There's not an actor in Hollywood who
doesn't want to generate the kind of deals commanded by Jack
Nicholson, and some would-be actors figure that by fathering a
child they will have something in common with the big stars—
perhaps they will even meet and network in Lamaze class.

The baby boomlet has changed the way business is conducted in Hollywood. Studios are combining acting classes
with prepared childbirthing courses. What has evolved from
this cross-collaboration of talent and hormones is Method
acting and Method child-rearing, mixing the best of
Stanislavski and Lee Salk. Classes include Dr. Salk on voice
projection and technique and Joe Pesci on prenatal care.

Top Hollywood agents are discovering that to keep their
famous clients, they need to offer both top representation and
baby-sitting services. Even outside the studios, the signs of a

Hollywood baby boom are everywhere. Birthing rooms in Los Angeles will soon be equipped with popcorn machines, stacks of Twizzlers, gallon buckets of Coke, and private screening rooms where stars can view tapes of their home deliveries. (This may start a spin-off trend. The *Hollywood Variety Reporter* recently reported that Carolco/Tri-Star offered Beatty and Bening over ten million dollars for the world rights to their taped coverage of the birth of Kathlyn Bening Beatty—with options on any further children the couple may conceive.)

On Rodeo Drive, the wealthy will soon be able to purchase Mercedes strollers, BMW car seats, Rolls-Royce prams, and Giorgio-scented baby oil. Ma Maison announced plans recently to open a day-care nursery during prime lunch hours. The baby boom has even affected the movies being shown in Hollywood. The famous Mann's Chinese Theater now premieres full-length cartoons. (No wonder *Beauty and the Beast* was nominated for a Best Picture Oscar!)

Hollywood's fascination with babies has altered some of our most basic concepts of pregnancy, the birth process, and child-rearing. In the 1950s, parents turned to Dr. Benjamin Spock for information and advice; his book, *Baby and Child Care*, sold twelve zillion copies. But sales began to wane in the early 1990s. "Dr. Spock's recognition quotient among the public had dropped to 37 percent," says his agent at ICM. "He could no longer carry a title on his own star power; he needed a buddy to recharge his likability with the folks in the suburbs. Hell, it worked for Danny Glover and Mel Gibson. The buddy movie is as old as Pablum in this town."

For this reason, publishers have recently released a sequel to *Baby and Child Care*, co-written by Dr. Spock and Leonard Nimoy. The new book combines the physician's comforting advice with the wisdom Nimoy has gleaned from his years as both a green-eared alien on national television and the director of *Three Men and a Baby*. In *Spock and Spock: Bringing Up Baby and Financing Your Script*, the authors write:

> The more people have studied different methods of bringing up children the more they have come to the conclusion that what good mothers and fathers instinctively feel like doing for their babies is the best after all—these methods seem even more appropriate when the parents themselves are rich and famous movie stars. For example, the perfect paternal role model is Clint Eastwood, who not only participated in raising his son, Kyle, but gave the kid a starring role in *Honkytonk Man*.

The following are examples from that forthcoming book, which is sure to become a bestseller and is soon to be a major motion picture.

Raging Pregnancy

Anticipating the unknown aspects of pregnancy frightens many women as their bodies, hormones, and emotions undergo massive changes. And the known side effect of pregnancy, though totally expected, is no less dreaded. Being pregnant means gaining weight, which really upsets a lot of women, especially older women who've battled with diets all their lives. Being a mother in your mid-thirties or early forties is traumatic enough; the thought of being grossly overweight can send many women over the edge.

Spock and Nimoy remind women not to worry about weight gain and advise them to compare this time in their lives with the time Robert De Niro gained fifty pounds to play Jake

La Motta in *Raging Bull.* The film was a major career boost, proving that sometimes it's okay to put on a few pounds for a good cause, be it to bring forth life or an Oscar nomination.

During the delivery, Spock and Nimoy offer this advice: "Practice your Lamaze breathing and your La Motta cervix-expanding exercises. Remember to breathe deeply, keep on pushing, and don't take any unnecessary punches to the head."

Don't Pamper Your Body with Pampers

This year, more than 16 billion disposable diapers will get buried in landfills. Roughly, that's 12,300 tons a day. This news is decidedly not good for you or your baby.

Babies using disposable diapers suffer more diaper rash than babies who wear cotton diapers. The superabsorbent chemical sodium polyacrylate in the disposable diaper's paper pulp is suspected of causing diaper rash. They do not degrade when buried in the landfill due to lack of light and oxygen. Also, their contents contain all kinds of viruses that can leach into the water table. As such, disposable diapers (what a misnomer, huh?) present a real hazard for the environment and pose a threat to the safety and well-being of future generations, not unlike the films of David Lynch.

Beverly Hills Day Care

New mothers and fathers have always had to struggle with the task of dividing the multitude of chores involved in raising a child. The stars in Hollywood have solved some of these problems in such creative ways that people in the nonacting community can really learn something from their example.

To prevent unseemly confrontations, Jack Nicholson and

Rebecca Brussard, the mother of his children, live in separate houses in Los Angeles, about a fifteen-minute drive from each other. Such a living arrangement is very helpful since it's really hard to argue with someone who's several miles away. Also, it helps alleviate the arguments about whose turn it is to use the bathroom.

Other Hollywood couples find it useful to keep the house well stocked with nannies, cooks, butlers, and at least three mother's helpers. Such a rudimentary staff will take away the drudgery of carpooling.

And remember that quality time is important. In Hollywood, quality time is between sunrise and seven-thirty A.M. and twenty minutes before sunset—when the lighting is at its most flattering. Be sure to share these moments with your child, especially if a photographer from *Vanity Fair* is present.

Another Hollywood father recently spent the ultimate quality time with his young child, sharing a moment when the child took his first steps. According to the actor's publicist, the actor and his child happened to be on Hollywood's Walk of Fame—that piece of sidewalk where stars' names are permanently embedded in cement. Reportedly, the child toddled his way from Lillian Gish to Lorne Greene.

HOOK Into Your Kid!

A child's first words are precious to his parents and you may want to have a tape recorder handy to record the event for posterity. Like parents around the world, mothers and fathers in Hollywood often make videotapes of their babies. This is done to preserve precious moments and to avoid lawsuits in the future. Before she died, Joan Crawford wrote an editorial in the *Los Angeles Times* bemoaning the fact that she hadn't made home movies of her daughter, Christina.

Encouraging your child to speak and teaching him or her the basics of proper English is important in your child's early education. Hollywood parents help their children in this area by providing voice coaches because, as Meryl Streep has often said, the sooner your child learns how to do dialects, the better his or her chances of becoming a major-motion-picture star.

Foreign-language skills are vital because you never know when Bertolucci may be casting in America. For this reason, many Hollywood parents hire domestic help from third-world countries.

According to many actors in Hollywood, it is never too soon to teach your child how to do impressions. After your child masters the rudimentary "Mama" and "Dada," you can move on to more specific dialogue such as "Fasten your seat belts, we're in for a bumpy flight!" and "I coulda' been a contender!" By the time your child is ready for kindergarten, he or she should be both toilet-trained and capable of impersonating John Wayne and one of the Three Stooges.

School Daze

Once your child has outgrown his diapers, formula, and bib, your parenting skills will really be put to the test. Your child will need a lot of personal attention from you to guide him or her through the difficult trauma of socialization, assimilation, and adapting to schoolwork. Prepare your youngster for that first day of school by watching *Kindergarten Cop* together. Remind your offspring that the first day of school is also your child's premiere appearance, his or her educational debut, so to speak. Tell the child what to expect by way of a dressing room and curtain calls.

Enjoy your child now because they grow up so fast. Before you know it, your second grader will be too busy to see you, especially between appointments with his or her personal trainer and his or her psychiatrist. Spend time with your child while he or she still has the time to spend with you. Childhood goes by so quickly, and it is the one thing in Hollywood that never goes into syndication.

Gloria Steinem's Self-Esteem Make-Over

Women suffer from a problem of self-esteem. We know this because Gloria Steinem just wrote a book saying we need to embrace our inner self; not just our inner child, but also our inner adolescent, our inner young adult, and the person we were twenty minutes ago.

We need to take all those inner selves, sit them down in one room, and say to each and every one of them, "I'm okay, you're okay. I love all of you. We are all doing the best we can although yesterday's inner self didn't need to finish that entire pizza by herself and last Friday's inner self shouldn't have insulted the boss."

Following this conversation, we are instructed to walk around the room and personally embrace each inner self. Learn to love all of the people you are, including the arrogant teenager whose carelessness with a toothbrush resulted in your recent gum surgery and the know-it-all hippie who got you hooked on smoking.

Learning to accept all of your inner selves is the first step toward gaining self-esteem. The second step is to have a complete make-over.

Looking well is not the best revenge, it's the only revenge. And looking better simply by buying a new tube of lipstick or a darker shade of eyeshadow is truly one of life's great pleasures. There isn't a woman alive who doesn't feel fantastic after discovering she can improve her looks without having to diet or undergo surgery. This is why women spent more than $4.7 billion on cosmetics in 1991 and, except for a few bottles of cerise nail polish, most women will confirm that it was worth every penny.

Looking young and attractive with makeup is the next best thing to actually being young and attractive. After all, a woman only has a few years where she really is youthful, but she can wear foundation makeup till the day she dies (and even after!).

Of course, women use makeup to attract men, and with good cause. Though the majority of men say women shouldn't use makeup because they're most attracted to the "natural look," these same guys always arrive at weddings with women who are made up like Vegas show girls.

The love of makeup begins quite early in life, possibly as young as the age of two, when children first become aware that Mommy spends an awful lot of time staring at her face in the mirror. Between the ages of three and four, little girls make the connection that Mommy is using some form of finger paint to enhance her appearance. Wanting only to imitate their mothers, little girls stare at their own reflections in the mirror until they finally reach the age when they're mature enough to realize that their lips could be a little fuller and their eyebrows need plucking.

By this time, around the age of six and a half, little girls are thinking about blushers and eye shadows; more mature six-year-olds begin questioning their mothers about the difference between perfume and toilet water. Many pediatricians have advised that once little girls begin to ask such questions, mothers should not be embarrassed to answer them as honestly as possible.

Notes one doctor: "Lying to your child about the price differential between toilet water and perfume can cause severe aroma confusion in future years. Later in life, your adult daughter may grow into one of those I-hate-perfume women who think natural odor is acceptable in public places."

Doctors also advise mothers not to place too much emphasis on makeup or you risk turning your daughter into a cosmetically dependent woman who hangs out at cosmetic counters of major department stores, begging salesgirls for free samples and overextending her welcome with the tester bottles. The cosmetically dependent can't pass a salesgirl holding a perfume bottle without receiving a free spray, often returning again and again. They spend their entire paycheck on home-shopping hair-care products. They live for Clinique giveaways. They collect flyaway perfume cards from fashion magazines. Often they can only have sex if their husbands or lovers are doused with Aramis.

The cosmetically dependent often get up an hour earlier than their spouses so that they're never seen without makeup. Many eventually chose a career with Mary Fay Cosmetics, where their addiction is not only accepted but encouraged. A former housewife and free-lance manicurist, Mary Fay built her company on her belief that a woman can never wear too much makeup or too many shoulder pads. "Show me a woman wearing tons of makeup, and I'll show you a woman who believes she looks great," Mary Fay says at the opening of her weekly sales meetings. "As Tammy Faye Bakker used to say, 'A woman without makeup is like a canvas without any paint—

who's interested?'" Though she may sound like a complete cotton-candy-head, Mary Fay's company is worth over $76 million.

The cosmetics industry was built on a simple principle. Makeup builds self-esteem by giving a woman two things she most needs to succeed in life: confidence and more prominent cheekbones. And when a woman looks good, who cares how she feels inside?

You Know You've Been in Therapy Too Long When...

1. Your bank account is down to $12.35.

2. Your doorman comments on the weather and you respond by asking, "And how do you *feel* about that?"

3. You start to cry whenever you flip your calendar to August.

4. You think every friend or acquaintance is interested in the time your mother forgot to attend your third-grade recital.

5. Your therapist falls asleep during one of your sessions.

6. You fall asleep during one of your sessions.

7. You start making phony phone calls, just to hear your therapist's answering service.

8. You begin every conversation with, "Well, my therapist says that..."

9. You don't cry anymore if your therapist takes a phone call during a session.

10. Your therapist relocates to another part of the country and you follow him or her.

11. You think of your therapist as your significant other.

12. You enter your boss's office for a meeting, head straight for the couch, lie down, and start talking about this weird dream you had last night.

13. You start liking your mother again.

14. You no longer care who your therapist is sleeping with.

15. You don't think it's funny when Woody Allen says to Diane Keaton in *Annie Hall*, "I've been in therapy fourteen years. I'm giving it one more year and then I'm trying Lourdes."

16. You run out of nasty things to say about your siblings.

17. You miss a session and your therapist doesn't notice.

18. You can't remember the year you started therapy.

19. You consider going back to school to become a therapist.

20. You name your firstborn child Sigmund.

How to Satisfy a Woman
30 Percent of the Time

Sex is a beautiful experience that can make you feel at one with the world and at peace with the cosmos. Sex is gratifying, stimulating, and good for your complexion. Sex is probably the most fun you can have in life without gaining weight or having a hangover the next day.

In this chapter we will explore several ways to increase your sexual pleasure and, for men, many valuable methods that will help you satisfy a woman 30 percent of the time, which, as all women know, is a miracle in its own right. This information can change your life because when sex is really good, it can even surpass the joy of finding a parking space on a rainy day.

The first way to have better sex is to find a partner. No matter how much you may enjoy having sex in the privacy of your own bathroom, sex can be even better when you do it with another person.

Secondly, sex can be more pleasurable when it's done with someone you love. Sex without love is often a depressing experience (although it is probably less depressing than being a virgin when you go through menopause). If you don't love your sexual partner, it is almost as good if you like him. If you don't like your sexual partner, then sex will only be good if you have a vivid imagination and a solid denial mechanism. Finally, if you cannot look at your sexual partner without thinking "I must really be desperate to sleep with this person," then it is advisable to keep your eyes closed during the entire sexual encounter.

Sex therapists have suggested that the best way to satisfy a woman is to tease her. The idea of teasing is to take your partner to the point where she is begging for more, and then to hold out just a little longer in order to increase the desire and, ultimately, the pleasure. "Teasing is a sweet form of torture and appeals to the masochist in everyone," says one famous sexologist who wishes to remain anonymous after his recent arrest for French-kissing a Dustbuster in a public place.

The soft tease can be effective in getting your partner ready for the main event. The soft tease involves creating a desire and making your partner suffer sweetly. To do this, you must be very gentle. Speak softly and carry a big sticky bun. Lick the icing off the sticky bun and say to your partner, "I know you've been on a diet all week, but this bun is soooo good. Mmmmmmm, yummy. You don't mind if I just eat this before we have sex, do you?" To really drive her completely crazy, you might also add, "Oh goody, raisins!"

Taking this teasing principle to the extreme can only increase your partner's pleasure. This is why some men who are really experienced lovers will arouse a woman just to the point of orgasm and then jump out of bed, get dressed, and say, "I'll call you next week."

If you really want to satisfy a woman 30 percent of the time, then you must be the one who takes control. Truly virile men know this instinctively, which is why a virile man never bothers to put the lid down on the toilet seat, ask for directions, or load the dishwasher.

A virile man, totally in control of the sexual encounter, will always want to be on top. He will be the one who determines where and when the sexual encounter begins and how quickly it ends. But men only *think* that they are in control, and women allow them that misconception because, at heart, women are more logical. Women know that in the race for gender superiority, they are in the forefront because only a woman can fake an orgasm with any real conviction.

From their very first sexual encounter, women learn this basic tenet: If you don't experience an orgasm during sex, then you have to fake it in order to save your partner's pride, build up his fragile ego, prevent arguments, and be polite. After all, men are generally much more insecure than women, and when they get hurt, they tend to turn mean and not return your phone calls.

If you don't fake an orgasm, then your sexual partner will almost certainly feel inadequate, and as you may know from work or from your mother, this is a very bad feeling. If you fail to convince your partner that you have had an orgasm, he may never want to have sex with you again, which will inevitably make *you* feel inadequate. So, you always want your sexual partner to feel like a tiger, even if you are frustrated enough to claw your way through your mattress and into the apartment downstairs.

In his book, *The Good-Enough Orgasm*, noted sexologist Dr. Seymour Knowmour points out that "Women should never feel guilty about faking an orgasm because, in my studies, I have discovered that 70 percent of all womanly orgasms are faked— or at the very least—spruced up to make a more convincing presentation. Of course, while this statistic is extremely unsettling to most men, I should add that contrary to what several disgruntled female book reviewers wrote about me, I have never personally known a woman to fake an orgasm. My personal percentage in bringing a woman to orgasm is 100 percent, and I have the videotape to prove it."

If you are still hesitating about faking an orgasm, remember this: If you don't fake an orgasm, your partner may accuse you of being frigid. This is a pejorative word that men like to use when they feel they aren't getting a satisfactory response from their sexual partner. In general, though, you will only be accused of being frigid by men who are lousy lovers, so don't take it personally.

When accused of frigidity, your best recourse is to stand your ground and be honest. Tell your partner, "I'm not frigid, just ask my tennis instructor." If that fails, do what women have been doing ever since virginity went out of style: fake it.

Faking an orgasm is easy once you learn how to do it. It involves four basic procedures: (a) loud moaning, (b) heavy breathing, (c) writhing around, especially with the lower half of your body, and finally, (d) verbal communication such as, "Oh baby. Do it to me, big boy."

Once you complete all four procedures, then you can stop all physical and verbal activity and go back to watching David Letterman. (If David has an especially interesting guest on that evening, you may want to speed up the process by skipping the writhing section. But do not let your sexual partner know that you are watching the television over his shoulder. And please, for God's sake, refrain from humming along with the commercials during intercourse.)

Faking an orgasm takes some practice, but you can get it if you try really hard. For inspiration, watch Meg Ryan's famous scene in *When Harry Met Sally* where she fakes an orgasm in Katz's Deli, and then try it yourself in your local coffee shop or Burger King.

After much practice, you will become proficient. Soon you

will be among the ever-increasing ranks of women who can fake multiple orgasms and balance their checkbooks at the same time.

To aid you in your fake orgasm, it is sometime helpful to engage in a fantasy. Many of us are shy about giving free rein to our fantasies, but this must be overcome. Do not be ashamed to let your imagination run wild during sexual intercourse; allow yourself the pleasure of imagining whatever you find most pleasing. Bette Midler, for instance, has invented a fine fantasy based on her husband's nationality. "My husband is German," she once said. "Every night I get dressed up like Poland and he invades me."

For most women, fantasizing involves pretending you are in bed with someone you find really sexy: Mel Gibson, Nick Nolte, Wayne Newton, or your gardener, for instance. Other women like to imagine being in an exotic location: a jungle in Africa, the conference room at the World Trade Center, a mountain top in the French Alps, the control tower of an airport, or the Calvin Klein department at Bloomingdale's.

Fantasies are fun because they are all yours and you don't have to share them with anyone. Some women like to fantasize that they are being photographed while making love, others enjoy the image of being tied up and having their legs waxed during intercourse.

Men should be aware that certain mechanical devices can also be used to increase a woman's sexual desire. Such devices include the BMW 735i convertible, the 35-inch cable-ready Sony Trinitron television with stereo speakers, and the GE washer and matching spin dryer.

Yes, sex is a divine experience, and contrary to what you may have been telling yourself, many people enjoy frequent sexual experiences. Just think: as you read this sentence, millions of people around the world are having sex *at this very moment*. If there's life on other planets, or life after death for that matter, then it's also possible that aliens in outer space and/or dead people are also copulating while you read this.

At any given moment, approximately 100 million people are having sex. This thought pops into my mind quite frequently. I'll be walking down the street or riding on the midtown bus during lunch hour, and I'll start to think about all the people who are having sex at that very moment. It makes me wonder at the vastness of the cosmos and makes me think, How come they're doing it and I'm stuck in traffic?

Sigmund Freud wrote, "Anyone who promises mankind liberation from the hardships of sex will be hailed as a hero, let him talk what nonsense he chooses." The lesson being, I suppose, that reading about sex won't teach you anything of value; sex is one subject that can only be grasped through field research. As Mrs. Alfred Kinsey once said, "I don't see much of Alfred anymore since he got so interested in sex."

Backlash or Whiplash?

The Undeclared War Against Single Women and Susan Faludi

In the 1970s single women were encouraged to pursue a career instead of a husband. By the 1990s, they were being assaulted for remaining single and for not having babies. Yes, being a single mother was accepted, even encouraged, by many people in society, with the glaring exception of anyone you knew personally who was a single mother.

The journalist Susan Faludi wrote about the backlash against single women, but she failed to mention the most prevalent physical manifestation of this condition: whiplash. Whiplash, which most victims describe as a severe and persistent pain in the neck, is caused by a single woman's conflicting ambitions to live an adult life but maintain a teenager's body. And maybe have a kid someday.

Several factors have foisted this problem on today's single woman. Radical changes in the women's movement have affected the economic climate, the cultural landscape, and most important, dating patterns between single men and women. These changes can best be documented by a close examination of the two most prominent female icons of the past two decades: Mary Richards and Murphy Brown.

Both of these fictional characters should be well known to all single women. Mary Richards was played by the phenomenally skinny though diabetic Mary Tyler Moore who, in real life, is married to a much younger doctor and lives in New York City. Murphy Brown is played by the former model/photojournalist/ serious person Candice Bergen who, in real life, is married to a famous French director, has a young daughter, and commutes between California and France.

Both of these TV characters set precedents for their day. Both Mary and Murphy are independent, single working gals who dress great and interact well with a crew of off-beat co-workers. Both work in television, although Mary worked behind the scenes in the newsroom while Murphy appears in front of the camera. However, Murphy pays a high price for her better job. She's got way fewer boyfriends than Mary, and not even her friends think she deserves one. These are only some of the similarities between Murphy and Mary. The following chart details the contrasts between these two characters, who exemplify the changes women have undergone in the past twenty years.

"As we moved from Mary to Murphy, the image of the working woman changed radically in this country," reports Professor Constance Crueller, who teaches "Women of the Sitcom: An Overview," at Bryn Mawr College. "Mary always called her boss Mr. Grant. She blushed and stammered if she had to ask him for a day off. Conversely, Murphy continually browbeats her boss, and often threatens to deflate his tires.

"Mary always had a flower on her desk as a symbol of her sweetness. Murphy can't keep a secretary, a metaphor for her short temper and unrealistic expectations. By today's standards,

---

SOCIOLOGICAL INDICATORS

<u>Mary Richards</u>   <u>Murphy Brown</u>

DECLINE IN MANNERS

Mary Richards	Murphy Brown
Spunky but good-natured	Spunky but ill-tempered
Stutters when nervous	Wisecracks; insults people when feeling vulnerable

SIGNS OF UPWARD MOBILITY

Mary Richards	Murphy Brown
Lives in small studio, later moves to one-bedroom apartment	Lives in an elaborate town house

RESULTS OF WOMEN'S ASSERTIVENESS

Mary Richards	Murphy Brown
Apologizes for everything	Never apologizes
Everyone loves her	Everyone hates her
Easily intimidated	Intimidating
Nice girl	Rhymes with rich

INCREASED REALISM ON TELEVISION

Mary Richards	Murphy Brown
No vices	Recovering alcoholic, former smoker
Took the pill	Got pregnant

Mary Richards would be considered a complete sap; she wouldn't last five minutes in Murphy's newsroom."

A big part of Murphy's problem with men stems from the so-called Man Shortage Epidemic, which wasn't invented until long after Mary Richards went into syndication.

The epidemic was first recognized in 1986, when the *Stamford Advocate* published results of a Yale study indicating that women who don't marry by the age of thirty had only a 20 percent chance of being wed; their odds went down to 5 percent by thirty-five, and after forty, well, junk those back issues of *Bride's Magazine* and burn grandma's wedding veil, it isn't going to happen.

The story of the epidemic was picked up by dozens of newspapers, talk shows, magazines, sitcoms, movies, self-help books, syndicated cartoon strips, greeting cards, and mothers of thirtysomething women across the nation. The survey caused severe anxiety and panic among single women, sending thousands stampeding to the personal ads, dating services, and whenever possible, down the aisle. The marriage rate increased a whopping 127 percent in the six months following the explosion of publicity about the man shortage.

The women who rushed to the altar (and many of them are currently in divorce proceedings) would later be surprised to discover that the study was, in fact, a complete misinterpretation of statistics. Investigations revealed the numbers were improperly crunched by three lonely statisticians who were hoping to make themselves appear more attractive to the female population in Connecticut. "A desperate woman is more likely to lower her standards," confessed one of the authors of the study. "We weren't out to hurt anyone, we just wanted a date for the Harvard-Yale game." They succeeded brilliantly. Within three months, each young man was involved in a serious relationship with at least two women. One was dating two roommates and flirting with a third.

In reality, there was no man shortage. Marriageable men existed. However, since the advent of cable television, they preferred to stay at home with their remote controls and 107 channels. Contributing to their alleged disappearance were several technological advances, including microwave ovens, fax machines, modems, VCRs, and half-hour delivery service from Domino's Pizza.

In point of fact, women were single because in overwhelming numbers, they were choosing not to marry, even when they had the opportunity. "What's the point of getting married?" asked one single woman from Chicago. "I can pump my own gasoline."

According to a poll by a major magazine, more than half the woman in the survey claimed they'd never remarry their current husband if they were given the opportunity (and many begged for the option). In another poll, when asked why they remained unmarried, more than 78 percent of the 60,000 single women surveyed said that instead of marriage, they much preferred their freedom, financial independence, and extra closet space.

It has been proven that marriage is, in fact, much more beneficial to men than women. Many statistics confirm that married men are more emotionally stable and less likely to experience nightmares, nervous breakdowns, or attempts at suicide than bachelors. The reverse is true for women. In general, single women are happier, healthier, and more physically fit than married woman. Also, single women generally have nicer clothes, longer vacations, less laundry, and more fun at parties than their married counterparts.

Still, some women chose marriage over the single life-style because, as one prominent psychologist told Sally Jessy, "Having a husband means never having to say you're sorry to your mother again. It's worth it." Sally Jessy agreed.

And so the debate continues to rage among women: Single vs. Married, Career vs. Family, Suits vs. Pants, Cellulite vs.

Liposuction, Sweet'n Low vs. NutraSweet, Valium vs. Xanax. Every day women are pulled in ten different directions. The multitude of options has given us a major case of whiplash.

We want to sue.

Many of us have law degrees and are ready to put our hard-won skills to maximum use. The question is: Whom to sue? The three statisticians who created the man shortage? The media that publicized it? The talk-show hosts and writers who continue to take advantage of those hateful statistics? The entire male gender? Just give us a name, we'll get the paperwork in motion.

The Ms. Middle-Aged America Pageant

This year, the Ms. Middle-Aged America Beauty Contest will be sponsored by the makers of Gyne-Ho-Chi-Min, the all-purpose household bathroom cleanser/feminine deodorant spray. "Women all across America will be invited to participate in the event," said a spokesperson for the product. "We hope to attract a whole new market of women aged 20 to 60 for our product, which has both professional and personal uses."

A national campaign to solicit contestants will soon appear in your local newspapers and in radio and television ads. To participate in the contest, potential applicants must fulfill the following criteria:

1. Must be female and able to prove it. Acceptable identification includes a driver's license, birth certificate, or photo ID from the local chapter of your Barry Manilow or Neil Diamond fan club.

2. Must be middle-aged. To determine if you are within the proper age range, simply take the total number of years you will be alive and divide by 2. Thus, if you will be dead at 40 because of that nasty smoking habit, you are middle-aged at 20

years old. Those who will live into their eighties, may not apply for the pageant until they are well into their forties.

Official Rules and Guidelines

Contestants will be judged in eight major categories: Swimsuit, Poise, Evening Gown, Marital Status, Career, Children, and Relationship with Mother.

Swimsuit: Contestants will not be judged on how well they look in a swimsuit since, as the Duchess of Windsor once said, "After a certain age, no woman should be seen without her diamonds or bathrobe." Instead, our lovely participants will be rated on their bravery and courage. Points will be awarded to the contestants who are willing to wear a bathing suit in public. Points will be deducted if the contestant wraps a towel around her waist.

Poise: We define poise as "grace under pressure," and the contestants will be judged by how well they maintain their composure when confined in a locked room with a whining child, a snotty salesclerk, and an irate ex-husband. Contestants will be awarded points for each minute spent in the room. Points will be deducted if the contestant bursts into tears, hurls a piece of furniture, or attempts to cause physical harm to anyone within fifty yards. Excessive sweating and cursing will also lower the contestant's total score.

Evening Gown: Contestants will be judged on their appearance in a formal evening gown. (Bridal dresses are not allowed.) Points will be added for any contestant wearing a great dress. By the rules of the contest, a "great" dress is one which makes the contestant appear ten pounds thinner than her normal weight.

Marital Status: The judges acknowledge that an important
aspect of a woman's life is her relationship with men, and
each contestant will be awarded points if she has one. Bonus
points will be granted if the contestant has a relationship
with a man who is not married, suicidal, excessively violent,
a blood relative, or currently dating more than two other
women. Contestants who are staying in a marriage or
relationship out of fear they can't do any better will be given
our sympathy and understanding but no points.

Career: The sponsors acknowledge the freedom of women to
choose whether or not to have a career. We do not wish to
offend either homemakers or careerists since both groups of
women purchase bathroom cleansers and feminine hygiene
products. Therefore, contestants will be awarded points for
either having a career or choosing to stay at home. However, there will be deductions. The career woman will be
penalized for not staying home and baking cookies with her
children. The housewife will be penalized for not going to
work and being financially independent. The career woman
will receive bonus points if she went free-lance or started her
own business before she got fired from her job.

Homemakers will be granted bonus points for volunteer
charity work, craft skills (sewing, knitting, plumbing, CPR),
and a working knowledge of the philosophy of Jean Auel.
Points will be deducted for homemakers who serve frozen
dinners, do not maintain a garden, or have not joined a
beach club.

Children: Applicants will be scored on the number of children
as well as on the table manners of each offspring. Bonus
points for each adopted child. Deductions for each child
with a criminal record. Childless women will not be
penalized, as they already receive enough flak from their
mothers. Women with more than four children will be

permitted to sit and put their feet up between events. *Relationship with Mother:* Contestants will be rewarded for maintaining an ongoing speaking relationship with their mothers. Points will be deducted, however, if the contestant's sister has a better relationship with mom. Bonus points will be added if the contestant took mom along during a family vacation or made her a surprise birthday party within the past five years. Deductions will be made for marrying beneath you, never listening to mom's advice, or taking your mother's name in vain on a call-in radio program.

Pageant Night

The Ms. Middle-Aged America Pageant will be broadcast live from the Shriners Auditorium in downtown Biloxi, Mississippi, the beauty-pageant breadbasket of America. Children will not be permitted backstage or within a twenty-five-mile radius of Biloxi. (Offshore baby-sitting services will be made available.) Husbands are also discouraged from attending the contest since they may cause unwarranted jealousy from some of the single contestants.

All applicants will be responsible for applying their own makeup and fixing their own hair. There will be no flirting with the judges, as most of them are homosexual and easily intimidated.

Every beauty pageant attracts its share of gawkers, geeks, and perverts, and ours is no exception. In fact, *The Mississippi Daily Register* once called the Ms. Middle-Aged America Pageant, "a magnet for otherly abled heterosexuals."

Although applicants are old enough to forgo supervision, we do advise extreme caution concerning selection and protection during off-hours. Discretion is advised. And remember that the television cameras can pick up a hickey at twenty feet.

Prizes

Our bandwagon of prizes for the lucky woman to be crowned Ms. Middle-Aged America include: a case of Gyne-Ho-Chi-Min, a $3,000 grant redeemable at over 2,500 plastic surgeons across the United States, a free periodontal checkup, a new pair of Pearl eyeglasses, a Watermark heating pad, two fifteen-minute electrolysis sessions, an appearance on *Live With Regis and Kathie Lee*, a rhinestone tiara, a dozen roses, and a large ribbon that reads MS. MIDDLE-AGED AMERICA.

Fashion Time Line

The following time line is an updated and expanded version of an idea suggested in 1937, by James Laver in *Taste and Fashion*. Laver made the point that the outfit doesn't change, we do. The same outfit, through the ages, will be:

FASHION TIME LINE

Indecent—10 years before its time
Daring—5 years before its time
Fabulous—½ hour before purchase
Flattering—tried on in dressing room
Perfection (with the right shoes)—tried on at home
Ultra chic—the first time worn
Smart—the second time worn
Borderline dowdy—after dry cleaning
Too tight—third time worn
Dowdy—1 year after its time
Hideous—10 years after its time
Ridiculous—20 years after
Amusing—30 years
Quaint—50 years
Charming—70 years
Romantic—100 years
Beautiful—150 years

Entertaining Without Martha

I find it harder and harder every day to live up to my blue china.

—Oscar Wilde, 1880

I love beautiful things. And I think I know what women really want...I have paid the highest price for my success. I really don't have a private life now...I give everything to my work, my fans.

—Martha Stewart, 1989
Yankee Magazine,
reprinted in *Woman* magazine

It has been well documented that entertaining in the 1980s was dominated by a woman named Martha, who taught us that the motive behind any party is the simple desire to impress someone who has less than you. (Why else does Martha insist that you display thirty-five hundred strawberries when you're entertaining six for dinner?)

But now, as we career headlong into a new decade with such cultural spokeswomen as Roseanne Arnold, the 1990s promise to redefine the art of entertaining. Krispin Detroit, editor of *Dinner Industry Standard,* a magazine that tracks dinner-party trends in urban and suburban settings, reports that "Ever since

Martha became the spokesperson for K Mart, our readers have begun to protest the basic tenets of Big M entertaining. They ask: Can I invite people to my house without subjecting them to mountains of crudités? Will I embarrass myself if I don't drape my table with a canvas sail? Will I be publicly humiliated for not owning a woven basket? Do I have to shop K Mart?" Obviously, hostesses around the country are rising up in protest. "The times are changing," claims Detroit, "especially dinner times."

Detroit cites these strategic indicators to support his thesis:

• Food has become more than an energy source for the body; it has assumed a psychological agenda. Serving butter today is making a firm statement to your guests: I do not care if your arteries are clogged.

• Scientific surveys have proven that the majority of people attend parties mainly as an excuse to go off their diet, drink too much, and smoke a cigarette. In the age of enlightened home entertainment and couch potatoes, people need positive motivation to get them out of their house and into yours. Door prizes are one solution.

• The proliferation of smog and the exhaust fumes from outdoor barbecues has caused many hosts and hostesses to forgo their traditional Father's Day and Fourth of July celebrations. As the Squiquillera family reported on the popular Los Angeles radio station, KRAT, "We was gonna throw Pop a barbecue, but the smog was so bad that day we couldn't find the lighter fluid."

The life-style bible of the next decade has been rewritten by those of us who like to entertain but haven't the time or money to renovate a Connecticut farmhouse. Here, then, are some of the basics you will need to know.

Party Preparations

Putting together a party is a lot like staging a Broadway show. Every aspect must be carefully orchestrated, beginning with location. Finding an appropriate setting in your home requires a fresh eye. For example, if your foyer will seat two hundred, don't hesitate to set up tables right there.

Of course, city dwellers who do not live in a floor-through apartment or town house may have to contend with some space restrictions, but such limitations should only serve to spur their imagination. I recently catered a lovely bridal shower on East 76th Street. We held the entire party in the future bride's linen closet. The cozy atmosphere really brought the guests closer together, and when anyone spilled anything, extra napkins where close at hand.

For less formal New York City parties, I like to entertain in the maid's room or broom closet. If the co-op board allows us access, we sometimes set up formal sit-down dinner parties in the building's freight elevator.

City kids love a birthday party set under the kitchen sink. All those pipes and outlets make kids feel like they are in a jungle gym.

In older prewar apartments, I have discovered that four to six guests can be comfortably seated in the fireplace.

Need a little more room? Squeeze an extra table into your bathroom. Tile floors provide great acoustics, especially if the entire band can squeeze into the bathtub.

For outdoor entertaining, balconies or rooftop decks have

become so commonplace that your guests will probably be bored to tears before the first course is served. Be inventive and release your own creativity! Arrange your next outdoor party on a window ledge or in a flower box. Your guests will be both amused and entertained once they master the technique of balancing themselves (and a hot barbecue grill) on a four-inch slab of concrete.

Also, be sure to decorate the entire entertaining area. At a recent picnic on Newport, I purchased four dozen pink plastic flamingos and scattered them across the oceanfront yard— adding a lively touch of pink to that endless backdrop of solid blue water.

Actually, I've discovered that pink plastic flamingos are perfect for almost every type of outdoor party. Unlike real birds, they also make perfect household pets. They never mess on the lawn, they don't need to be fed, and they can't fly away. (I wish I could say as much for my last husband!)

Hired Hands

Hiring help for your party is an absolute necessity. As far as I am concerned, one can never have too much help. As the Duchess of Windsor once said, "You can never be too rich, too thin, or too overstaffed." And she was a lady who required her servants to iron her bed sheets before and *after* making her royal bed. (It's no wonder that the Duchess is often credited by biographers as being one of the original Martha Mentors.)

For my own parties, however, I am too economical to pay professional bartenders and waiters, so I usually rely on my friends and family to help out because they wouldn't dream of asking for money. Of course, Mom gripes a lot about all the work, especially after that accident where she broke her hip, but I refuse to give in to her complaints. "Mom," I always tell her, "you *can* do it if you try. We'll just prop this tray of canapés on your walker and off you'll go!"

Last-Minute Preparations

- Take a shower if you tend to perspire under pressure.
- Lock your phone so none of your guests can make long-distance calls.
- Hide all personal hygiene products. Remember that even the classiest guest will not be able to resist the temptation to inspect your medicine cabinet. (A day or two before any party in my house, I always make sure that my Valium supply is locked away in my safety deposit vault.)
- Small children and pets should be sent to stay with friends or relatives who weren't lucky enough to get invited to the party.
- A friend of mine ties a big turquoise ribbon, banister to banister, across the stairway leading to her bedroom. This tells her guests: *Stay Out of My Private Quarters* and *I Once Got a Really Expensive Present from Tiffany's.*

Making Your Guests Feel at Home

The caring hostess will take special pains to ensure that her guests feel welcome and loved. Being attentive to your guests means knowing how to spot those times when they feel uncomfortable. Here are some telltale signs:

- A guest refuses to relinquish coat or briefcase.
- She stares longingly at your front door.
- He watches television and refuses to make room for you on the couch.
- He locks himself in your basement.

There are several solutions to these awkward entertaining dilemmas. First, to make a guest feel more comfortable in your home, ask him or her to join in the preparations for the evening. If I think a guest is feeling a bit out of place, I ask him or her to help with a simple chore like vacuuming the carpet or scrubbing the bathtub.

After my guests have finished their chores, I like to bring them into the kitchen, where I am usually busy with my last-minute cooking preparations. In the warmth of the kitchen, I occupy my guests with good conversation and offer them sample tastes of the course to come. This makes my job of preparing dinner a bit more complicated, but I do it to make my guests feel at home and because I keep hoping that one of them will be able to fix my broken dishwasher.

If anyone offers to help with the dinner preparations, I don't hesitate for a moment. I send them directly to the supermarket with my weekly shopping list and a stack of redeemable coupons.

During the course of any party, a time may come when things start to drag and there's a lull in the conversation. Ask yourself: Has someone fallen asleep between courses and interrupted my other guests with his snoring? If you answer yes, it means you need to breathe some life into your guests. You can liven up the evening by surprising your guests: change seating arrangements between courses, serve wild boar, announce that your house is on fire, or pass out during the main course (even more fun—pass out *in* the main course!).

As a hostess, you have certain obligations to your guests. For example, you should hang around the party. This is no time to catch a revival of *Lawrence of Arabia* at your local movie theater. Your guests will expect you to be present, at least until dessert is served. After that, it is permissible to disappear for an hour or two if you have some personal banking that needs your attention.

One of my fondest memories is the party where Marlena, our hostess, spent the entire evening in the bathroom, leaving us, her guests, to fend for ourselves with the meal. We were worried sick about her health as we ate everything in her refrigerator and then ransacked her bedroom bureaus. (I found an Hermès scarf I'd lent her two months ago.) You can imagine our relief to discover, at the end of the evening that Marlena wasn't sick, she'd simply been having sex in the bathtub with her sister's boyfriend and forgotten the time.

As Marlena discovered, entertaining in the 1990s can be fun, rewarding, and sexually gratifying. Those of us who grew up in the sixties had forgotten the value of entertaining. Thank goodness Martha came along to remind us that a life-style is a terrible thing to waste.

Call Waiting...

The way we live today is drastically different from the era of Mouseketeer ears and backyard bomb shelters. I know because I'm a Baby Boomer, and I've seen the world change in odd and mysterious ways. Young people today don't understand how different it was, back before cash machines and cable television. I started dating, for example, long before there was call waiting or answering machines. In my day, we had something called "a busy signal," which meant that you had to hang up and call again. And forget speed dialing or memory storage. You had to remember the seven-digit number and dial it yourself on a labor-intensive rotary phone—it took forever for each number, especially the 9 and the 0.

Of course, answering machines and call waiting have all but eliminated the busy signal. Ironically, the early answering machines were not well received. Callers were annoyed to have the phone answered by an impersonal mechanical object. Many would refuse to leave a message, hang up, and later complain that it was rude to expect them to talk to a machine. Country music songs, such as "Please Leave a Message When You Hear the Beep, Creep" or "I'm Leaving You a Message You Don't Want to Hear," expressed the public's outrage.

Today, of course, callers are annoyed if the phone *isn't* answered by a machine. "Many people have forgotten how to talk to a real live person on the phone," explains Dr. Krime A. River of the Georgia Institute of Long-Distance Dialing. "They prefer to call when no one is home just so they can leave their message and hang up." In fact, many long-term relationships between friends, family, and business associates are conducted solely through contact from machine to machine. One couple in Des Moines, Iowa, maintained an entire relationship through phone messages, never actually meeting in person or talking to each other on the phone. "It was great while it lasted," reported the woman, who wished to remain anonymous. "He had a very nice voice, and when I came home from work and saw that light blinking on my machine, I really enjoyed the illusion that I was involved in a relationship."

Some people consider the answering machine the most important invention since the Salk vaccine and cannot imagine life without one. Others are annoyed that the machine is completely indiscriminate, preserving the important messages and the obscene phone calls without distinguishing between the two. That may change in the future. Scientists are developing software which will program your answering machine to hang up on selected people, particularly blood relatives and members of the legal profession.

Today's machines come equipped with a wide variety of technological advancements. Some machines are capable of announcing the date and time the phone message was recorded, making it not only useless but embarrassing for the caller to lie about when he or she called. More sophisticated equipment is about to appear on the market. A new model, the CODE-A-PHONY XR431, combines the technology of message retrieval with the accuracy of a lie detector. When the message is played, a slip of paper emerges from the machine with a line graph indicating the places where the caller is lying. First tested by consumers during the summer of 1992, the XR431 has proven particularly popular with single women who date married men.

Single men and women were the first consumers to sign up for call waiting, and this service has subsequently created an entire etiquette of its own. When you hear that click in the middle of a conversation, proper procedure is to excuse yourself, putting your caller on hold, while you find out who is on call waiting. It is always correct to take a message from the new caller and return to the original caller as quickly as possible. The first caller always has precedence over the new caller except when the new caller is (a) offering you work or money, (b) calling from more than three thousand miles away, or (c) is either 46 percent more interesting or 37 percent better looking than your original caller.

The rules concerning the proper etiquette for dealing with car phones are still being written since the technology is relatively rudimentary. In most cases, car phones are meant more to impress than inform, since static and interference severly hinders any real communication. It has been my experience when talking to someone on a car phone that the minute the conversation veers toward anything you really want to hear, the caller drives into a tunnel. For this reason, the rules of proper phone etiquette do not apply to car phoners. Once I was having a conversation with this guy on his car phone when he suddenly hung up on me. I was really annoyed until I later learned that he wasn't being rude, he'd been rear-ended while waiting at a red light.

Car phones and mobile phones are important status symbols, especially in California where portable phones are used as fashion accessories. One designer calls his hanging cellular-phone necklace "the most important jewelry statement since the tennis bracelet." Look for digital-phone earrings and cellular-hat phones in the not-too-distant future.

Equipment has become ever more important and complicated in our lives. Recently, I worked in an office that held weekly classes to teach employees how to operate their telephone, voice mail, and computer mailbox. In my day, incoming employees were handed a directory of office extensions, an in/out box, a box of pencils, and a stapler.

It is interesting to note, though, that as adult toys get ever more complicated, children's toys are returning to the simple, inexpensive items Baby Boomers loved when they were kids. Indicators of this trend include increased sales in jacks, jump ropes, marbles, Trolls, Creepy Crawlers, Barbie dolls, G.I. Joes, and Scrabble. Sean P. McGowan, a toy industry analyst with Gerard Klauer Mattison & Company was quoted in the *New York Times* as saying, "I find it ironic that the women who burned bras will buy Barbie dolls in droves for their kids, and the generation of men who burned their draft cards are buying G.I. Joes."

Actually, the explanation for this dicotomy is simple. The parent who spends three hours learning how to make an outside call or retrieve her voice-mail message has only a limited amount of time to play with her child, so she wants to avoid the complicated instructions or directions involved for toys that simulate thermodynamic flight or intensive surgical procedures. A quiet game of marbles or staging a Barbie tea party is perfect playtime between Baby Boomer and child.

In the future, quality time will be defined as the allocated time slot when parent and child interact without benefit of batteries, joystick, or keyboard, which was, ironically, pretty much how parents did it back in my day.

Carolyn Warmus and Amy Fisher Reveal Everything You Didn't Want to Know About Dating a Married Man

Inevitably, at some point in a woman's dating career, she will be tempted to have an affair with a married man. Some women consider this a rite of passage, others call it kamikaze dating.

No one can tell you whom to date (you wouldn't listen anyway), but before you decide you're mature enough to handle a little weekend in the Bahamas without getting emotionally involved, read this chapter carefully. Much of this material was gathered from testimony by Caroline Warmus and Amy Fisher. Though they never met, Warmus and Fisher share a common bond. Both fell in love with married men and were driven so crazy that they tried to murder their boyfriend's wife. Warmus scored a direct hit (or, rather, eight direct hits); Fisher caused permanent physical damage. Both women are now serving time.

Caroline and Amy have become the nation's leading experts in the field of interpersonal relationships between unequal partners. Now, for the first time, they reveal the Indisputable Facts About Dating a Married Man. This information is presented as a public service with the hope that before you pack that suitcase, you'll keep in mind the rising cost of psychotherapy and legal representation.

1. It's going to end badly.
No matter how it starts, the relationship will end with both a bang and a whimper.
He'll get the bang, and you'll get to whimper.
Both of you will be miserable, of course, and suffer in your individual ways. The only difference is he'll be comforted by the presence of his wife and children, and you'll turn to a bunch of friends and relatives who'll offer words of support while quietly humming "I told you so."

2. You'll honestly believe that he is totally different from the married men your friends are seeing. When other women tell you they believe their married boyfriends do not sleep with their wives anymore, you'll think your friends are pathetically naive. At the same time, you'll be totally convinced that your married boyfriend is completely faithful to you.

3. You will continue to believe that some day he will marry you, even years after you've stopped seeing him.

4. You will be miserable on holidays, national or personal. Weekends will seem interminably long. You will cry easily and often over television commercials, especially the one that tells you to "reach out and touch someone." You will blame yourself for his not leaving his wife, thinking that if only you were more attractive, smarter, thinner, sexier, kinder, and more patient, he would now be lying next to you in bed.

5. As the years progress, it will take an ever-increasing amount of energy to keep your optimism operating.

6. The sex will be fantastic. Married men compensate for all the stuff they don't give you by being great lovers. It's one of their most charming characteristics and one of the few true advantages of dating someone else's husband.

7. Married men also compensate by buying you expensive gifts and taking you to four-star restaurants and hotels. If nothing else, an affair with a married man will greatly enhance your collection of lacy lingerie, though your cholesterol level may increase by as much as 30 percent.

8. He's not going to leave his wife.
   "This cannot be said often enough," says Caroline.
   "Get used to hearing it again and again," agrees Amy.

9. Don't feel secure if he does leave his wife, because the odds are he won't marry you anyway (now known as the Marla Maples syndrome). You'll be the one who helps him through the separation, the divorce, and the settlement, so you'll always remind him of his ex-wife. You will be his transition woman.
   Here's what will happen: As soon as he signs the divorce papers, he realizes he's finally free and he wants to experience his single life. He leaves you, and three months later marries the next woman he dates. Why? Being new to the singles market, he will panic easily. He will date several women. Soon he is overwhelmed, terrified about being alone and frustrated over having to handle the emotional needs of more than one female.
   He will solve the problem by making a commitment to the

woman he feels is least like his former wife. She will have an 87 percent chance of marrying him, barring any unforeseen complications such as unemployment or impotence.

10. He will be the last married man you will ever date.

Women on the Verge
of Bankruptcy

Women today are more self-sufficient than ever before. We have learned how to support ourselves, to take responsibility for our financial security, to stop depending on daddy or hubby to pay our bills. Consequently, we are now just as much in debt as men.

"There is no sexism in the bankruptcy courts," jokes the esteemed financial adviser, Dr. Eleanor Kuklah-Gross. Known to her friends and colleagues as Dr. EKG, the good doctor actually began her careeer as a geriatrician, working with the terminally ill. In her first landmark book, *Dead People's Society*, Dr. Kuklah-Goss charted her patient's progress from "Doctor, I don't feel so good today" to "Quick, call the priest!" She identified five stages in the dying process—denial, anger, bargaining, depression, and acceptance—which she termed the DABDA Movement. Her work was rewarding but ultimately routine. "After several years, it became apparent to me that eventually everybody dies," the doctor said in a recent interview. "That realization totally eliminated the surprise element from my work."

It was a turning point in her career. Dr. EKG decided to

diversify. She enrolled in a night-school accounting course. She studied hard and, after several years, became a CPA. The doctor opened an accounting office in the hospice where she practiced. "Death and taxes," she told a colleague. "I figured I'd always make a living."

After many tax seasons, Dr. EKG began to notice that her five stages of grief, the DABDA Movement, applied not only to the dying, but to every woman who was the head of her own household. And, as the economy continued to plummet, more and more women seemed to undergo a similar transformation from giddy credit-card charger to anxiety-ridden debtor.

"The moment that a woman is told she's in serious financial trouble, she reverts to the classic, stage-one state of *denial*," Dr. EKG reported in a paper she delivered during the annual company picnic at the H & R Block headquarters. Dr. EKG went on to explain that the first sign of the onslaught of this stage is when a woman says to herself, Sure I can afford these Nikes, especially since they're on sale for ninety-five dollars.

She charges the sneakers and enjoys wearing them until the bill arrives. Checking her MasterCard statement, she looks only at the interest charge and thinks, I can afford a hundred fifty dollars this month.

What about the total debt of seven thousand dollars? I'll definitely pay some of that next month, she tells herself, even though subconsciously, she has no intention of ever paying more than her minimum interest payment due. She completely blots the total debt from her mind. The woman is in denial.

Denial only lasts for so long, according to Dr. EKG. Pretty soon even the interest payments are making a huge dent in her monthly total. That's when *anger* sets in. The helpless woman is furious about the bad luck that's brought her to the brink of financial ruin, despair, and/or suicide. Some women have become so infuriated during this stage that they refuse to recycle, defiantly tossing their aluminum cans and glass bottles in the garbage with selfish abandon.

Guilt soon takes over. She's rinsing out those diet Coke cans and entering stage three: *bargaining.* "Please don't let me go bankrupt. I'll be good," she pleads to some silent higher banking power. "No more facials for six months. I won't buy another thing till Christmas. I'll cancel the mammogram appointment; it's so disgusting anyway. Just please, I don't want to lose the gold AmEx card." Bargaining techniques during this period include using public transportation, shopping at Loehmann's, eating salads at home for dinner, fewer CDs, and no new magazine subscriptions.

All of these examples of self-control and deprivation eventually lead to stage four: *depression.* Is there any need to define the word *depression* to any person with access to a talk show, magazine, or newspaper?

Dr. EKG issues a word of warning concerning the penchant of some women in the depths of stage four to visit a therapist, supposedly to find a cure. A recent exit poll at a mental-health clinic on 105th Street and West End Avenue in New York City asked several patients to choose between feeling (a) manic depression or (b) acute anxiety. Nine times out of ten, they chose manic depression.

"I used to think being depressed was the worst thing in the whole world," reported one woman, who wished to be called Sirhan. "But then I got cured. Five years of therapy and I no longer get into those suicidal depressions where I'd stay in bed and cry all afternoon, watching movies on my VCR and talking with friends for hours. Now, I really miss those days because without the depression, man, I have to deal with everything. I'm a bundle of nerves, up all night watching Letterman and eating ice cream. I never lost a night's sleep as a manic depressive. In fact, I never lost an afternoon's sleep either."

Coping with the absence of depression is difficult, but once the patient has come through the tunnel, she discovers that the flip side of depression is *acceptance*, the final destination through her financial grief. During this stage, she accepts her financial limitations and gets a job, gets married, asks for a raise, borrows money from her parents, or takes out a second mortgage. She accepts the fact that in the 1990s, sooner or later, everyone will be in debt up to their eyebrows. "Death and debt, you can't escape the inevitable," warns Dr. EKG.

The only real relief is for a woman to accept the spiritual side of her financial burdens. She must learn to live with her poor credit rating and embrace her debts with love and forgiveness. "In the next few years, the prayer mat will replace the money machine as a symbol of peace, harmony, and community," predicts Dr. EKG. "That's the reason why I've opened a prayer-mat factory at the hospice. The old-timers are great at weaving, they rarely complain about being paid minimum wage, and most of them are gone by the time I have to post their FICA deductions. I hope the spiritual movement continues to revolutionize this country. It's incredibly lucrative!"

The Princess and the PMS

I Wouldn't Settle for a Prison Cell, Would You?

Once there was a very wealthy real-estate mogul who wanted to marry a princess, but she had to be a *real* princess. He traveled all over the Upper East Side where he found many princesses, but whether they were real princesses was difficult to discern. True, they all dressed like princesses in their Chanel suits and Ferragamo shoes, and certainly, they all acted like princesses by ordering the lobster salad with balsamic dressing when chicken salad was half the price. But still, there was always something not quite right about them. They overtipped or spoke too kindly to cab drivers. They claimed empathy for the working class, or they supported food stamps for the poor. They didn't care about interest rates, or they voted Democratic.

So finally the mogul returned to his palatial hotel in mid-Manhattan and ordered the lights dimmed on his big Empire Tower, which let everyone in the kingdom know he was very unhappy because he wanted a real princess so badly.

One evening there was a terrible thunderstorm in the mogul's beloved city. The power lines went down, the phones went out, and the palace basement was flooded with water. Room service was two hours late, and housekeeping ran out of dry towels.

In the middle of this frightful storm, someone knocked on the door of the mogul's penthouse, and because the servants were all busy lighting candles or trying to press the mogul's pants with hot bricks, the mogul answered the door himself.

It was a princess who stood in the hallway, but she was in a very bad mood because of the storm. Her Chanel suit was soaking wet and her Ferragamo suede pumps were ruined beyond repair.

"What the hell's going on here?" she screamed. "The concierge says he gave away my room. I can't get a drink at the bar. My hairdo is absolutely destroyed. What kind of palace are you running? I had a reservation and besides, I'm a princess!"

"A real princess?" asked the Mogul.

"Everything about me is real, buster," she said, poking her finger in the mogul's chest, "with the expection of my breasts, a couple of fingernails, and this hair weave which used to be attached to my head."

"Well, we'll soon see whether she's a *real* princess," thought the mogul to himself.

He ordered his butler to prepare a room. The mogul's instructions were very specific: Put a pea on the bed frame and then pile twenty mattresses on top of the pea. On top of the mattresses, the butler was to pile twenty down quilts.

In the morning the mogul asked her, "Did you sleep well?"

"Are you serious?" she replied. "I barely closed my eyes. Where do you buy your mattresses? In Beirut? I'm black and blue all over from lying on something so uncomfortable. You'll be getting a bill from my orthopedic surgeon in the morning, and count yourself lucky if I don't sue. And what's more, buster, there was no makeup mirror in my bathroom. The ice bucket was empty. There were fingerprints on my water glass. I chipped a nail on the closet door. The desk was out of stationery. There was no phone in the hall closet. And the only thing playing on cable television was a Chevy Chase movie."

The mogul saw at once that she must be a real princess, either that or she was premenstrual. He asked her to stay for another month just to be sure. Every morning she awoke with a batch of fresh complaints: The toilet ran all night. The floorboards creaked. The towels weren't fluffy enough. The bathroom mirror made her complexion sallow. The washcloths didn't match. The complimentary shampoo gave her a rash. The faucet leaked. There was soap scum on the shower curtain. There weren't enough hangers. The laundry bag was too small. Pages were missing from her Gideon Bible. The radiator clanked and the air conditioning wasn't cold enough. Her wake-up call was two minutes and thirty-seven seconds late. The water pitcher wasn't Waterford. Room service forgot her marmalade. The complimentary bar didn't stock Tab. The bellboy sneered when she refused to tip him. The chamber-maid couldn't dust her way out of a paper bag.

"That's enough!" said the joyful mogul. "It isn't PMS, you are a *real* princess!"

So the mogul married the princess and made her a real queen.

In her first official act, she fired everyone on the mogul's staff, redecorated the palace, and took charge of the mogul's accounting department. She restructured the entire kingdom and saved the mogul a bundle of money by cutting down on employee benefits such as health care, bonuses, pay increases, and unemployment benefits. She sliced dental care and maternity leaves for the entire staff. She stopped paying for such extravagances as Social Security and FICA.

At first, the mogul tried to control her since she was getting to do all the fun stuff, but she yelled louder and fought dirtier, so, gradually, he stopped coming into the office. Staying at home, counting his increasing piles of gold, silver, and IRAs, he slipped deeper and deeper into reclusive behavior which his doctors claimed was senility. The queen filed for Medicaid benefits on his behalf.

One day the IRS arrived and took the queen to court, charged with fraud, tax evasion, and rudeness. The mogul was deemed too senile to stand trial.

The queen hired the most expensive attorney in the land. "My client suffers from PMS envy," the attorney claimed in the queen's defense. "The medical community defines this condition as an irrational jealousy of any woman still young enough to menstruate. In the queen's case, the envy is so intense that it causes her to act greedy and insensitive."

"She doesn't need a jail sentence," her psychiatrist testified. "She needs counseling and massive doses of intravenous Midol."

The queen personally pleaded for mercy from the judge. She wept, she fainted, she developed heart palpitations, she threatened to commit suicide. She offered to build hotels for the homeless. The judge claimed the rich couldn't buy their way out of jail, which came as a real shock to the queen's attorneys.

The queen was sentenced to four years in a minimum-security prison. Once she was incarcerated, the warden told the local paper that because of the queen's experience operating the palace, she might qualify for a job mopping floors or washing bed sheets.

The queen was not amused. She spent her jail time on her cellular phone, operating the palace from her cell. But, in absentia, she was soon voted off the board of directors and lost control of her empire. Her name was removed from all the business stationery, and her photo was scraped off the palace dinner plates.

Now she spends her days and nights plotting her revenge. She plans to sue the IRS, the judicial system of New York State, everyone who testified against her, the prison warden, the media, and her cellmate, who smokes a pack of Camels a day and bathes infrequently.

Meanwhile, the king emerged from senility ("a miracle cure," reported his legal counsel) and has since filed divorce papers. According to local gossip columnists, he is looking for a new princess. Recently, he was spotted lunching at La Grenouille with Ivanarella.

Lying Like Leona

Leona H. went to prison for lying on her income-tax returns. Okay, she claims she wasn't really lying, although she might have stretched the truth a fraction.

No matter what your two cents are worth, Leona H. was judged harshly by the press. She was called the Queen of Mean, among many other nasty things. People were ruthless in judging her and supporting a severe punishment. Personally, she wasn't someone I'd want as a friend or employer, but I think she got a raw deal. After all, aren't we all guilty of a similar crime? Which of us hasn't fudged just a little bit on a tax return? (Not me, of course, but many have.)

On the issue of honesty, men and women seemed quite divided. After a brief survey among friends and colleagues, I can say with absolutely no scientific basis, but a very strong hunch, that lying comes easier to men than it does to women.

Men think of themselves as honest and forthright, yet they recognize the necessity of lying to protect their interests in certain circumstances. Usually, they lie to avoid hurting someone close to them, say, a wife or mistress. Thus, lying is an act of love, according to the way most men see it.

Men, especially the ones I date, have always said that

everyone needs a few healthy white lies to get through the day, otherwise we might not get out of bed in the morning.

Women do not lie as easily as men. And they feel so guilty when they do tell a lie that they wind up apologizing to whoever will listen. If no one will listen, they hire a therapist and pay for listening services. Women do excel, however, at lying to themselves.

When they say life is seamless and the circle is complete, this is what they mean: Men lie to women and women lie to themselves.

To prove the point, here's a little test. Listed below are women's most common everyday lies. Read through this list and check the boxes for lies with your name on them. Score one point for each check mark.

- [ ] I used to be a perfect size six.
- [ ] I haven't eaten a thing all day.
- [ ] The dry cleaners shrunk these pants.
- [ ] There are no available men out there.
- [ ] I broke up with him.
- [ ] I'll start my diet on Monday.
- [ ] I'm not the jealous type.
- [ ] I *never* gossip.
- [ ] He wasn't right for me.
- [ ] I never eat dessert.
- [ ] Sex isn't that important.
- [ ] I never read the personal ads.
- [ ] I don't regret anything.
- [ ] I'm too busy to exercise this morning.
- [ ] I don't like possessive men.
- [ ] I only want a bite of yours.
- [ ] I'd never consider plastic surgery.
- [ ] I thought this space was legal.

☐ I don't need therapy.
☐ I could have gotten married lots of times.
☐ I never watch TV.
☐ I must be retaining water.
☐ I'm never jealous of my friends.
☐ I'm nothing like my mother.
☐ I don't believe in horoscopes.
☐ This is my natural color.
☐ I don't need glasses.
☐ I never lie about my age.
☐ I'm not ready to get involved.
☐ I used to smoke three packs a day.
☐ He'll change after the wedding.
☐ I never wanted to be a cheerleader.
☐ He'll leave his wife.
☐ No one will notice if I don't shave my legs today.
☐ I never lie.

SCORING:

More than 30 check marks proves that you're a liar. Fewer than 30 check marks proves that you're a liar. Move over, Leona.

Excerpts From the Diary of a Mad Single Woman

Dear Diary: I'm remembering happier days, before cellulite was invented. Things are not so good. The only bright spot this week was on my X-ray...

Dear Diary: Just saw this Levi's jeans commercial on television. A really cool guy looks into the camera and says, "I know who I am. And that's what's good about me." I have a negative response to this ad. I think it's humiliating when a television commercial is more profound than the man I love.

Dear Diary: Over dinner Ken said, "There's this couple in my building who are like in their eighties. She swims fifty laps a day, he jogs. They're always off on some exotic trip to Africa or Tahiti. They went cross-country in a van last summer. You know, I only hope I'm as active when I get to be their age."

"But, Ken," I said, "you don't do that kind of stuff now. What makes you think you'll do it thirty years from now?"

His friends laughed, but he gave me a very dirty look. And he hasn't called in two weeks. Did I say something wrong?

Dear Diary: After living with Richard, I discovered that men are only good at cleaning stuff they can hose down…Just read a story about a couple in St. Cloud, Florida, who signed a suicide pact. She shot herself with a .38 pistol; he watched her die and then changed his mind. He strapped her in her seat belt and drove to a friend's house, which should serve as a reminder to all women to be skeptical of this "ladies first" business we're always hearing.

Dear Diary: The royal family. What a bunch of characters! Ironic, because when I was a little girl growing up in New Jersey, I always dreamt of one day marrying Prince Charles and becoming the first Jewish Queen of England. That dream was shattered, of course, when he married Di, but now that the marriage seems to be on the rocks…I wonder. Should I book a trip to London this winter? I told Mark that Christmas in London would be just like Dickens, and he said, Yeah, orphans starving in the street, people going to the poor house…Maybe I'll try Barbados instead…

Dear Diary: Give me the strength and courage to live my life One Meal at a Time…

Dear Diary: I'm so discouraged. Nothing I write ever sells. My editor says the only way to make money in this business is to write a biography of Princess Di, Marilyn Monroe, or Jackie Kennedy Onassis. But won't that involve library research?

Dear Diary: What happened to the space program? We went to the moon while the Japanese built VCRs, which is why they own all the real estate today. It took a genius to figure out that Americans would be more interested in *Police Academy 4* than in moon rocks?…I don't get this idea of why anyone would be interested in Virtual Reality. Isn't Actual Reality bad enough? Do we really want to duplicate it?

Dear Diary: I think someone should invent a car that folds up into a suitcase so that when you arrive at your destination you don't have to find a parking space…

Also, a washing machine that converts itself automatically into a dryer after the spin-dry cycle so you don't have to transfer the clothes from one machine to another.

I could be a millionaire if I knew how to make stuff and wasn't afraid of electricity.

Dear Diary: I'm now convinced that, in the future, everyone will host their own talk show for fifteen minutes…

Dear Diary: Why isn't there a law prohibiting parents from putting pierced earrings on infants? In a truly civilized country, the government would establish a minimum legal age for accessorizing.

Dear Diary: Is it my imagination or are there more scandals these days than ever before? A brief list comes to mind: Ivan Boesky, Michael Milken, Leona Helmsley, Mike Tyson, William Kennedy Smith, Donald Trump, Clarence Thomas, Robert Maxwell, Rob Lowe, the entire royal family, and every presidential candidate.

People are obsessed with public scandals. The Germans call it *schadenfreude,* which roughly translated means "malicious glee over the misfortune of others." Evidently *schadenfreude* has become yet another epidemic of the nineties.

I often ask myself, How would I feel if my personal life was splashed across the front page of the *New York Post*? I can just imagine the headlines:

HASN'T CALLED MOTHER IN SIX WEEKS
ATE TWO GOOD HUMOR POPS BEFORE GOING TO BED
JEALOUS OVER BEST FRIEND'S ENGAGEMENT

Reading this list sends a shiver down my spine. I must try to get a more interesting life...

Dear Diary: I just finished editing two gift books, *It's a Boy!* and *It's a Girl!*, which celebrate the miracle of birth through photographs and quotes about mothering and child-rearing. I was warned By the publisher that I could not include any photographs of naked infants, even if the picture showed only a glimpse of a newborn's backside. "We're nervous about the Mapplethorpe scandal," the editor told me. "We don't want to offend anyone." By the same token, movies and television shows have become ever more sexually explicit. How can the image of a newborn lying on a blanket be considered pornographic when naked women openly spread their legs on public-access cable-television shows?

Dear Diary: A quick survey of the bestseller charts today indicates that women (who make up the majority of book buyers) have two major concerns: menopause and the unhappy life of Princess Di. Imagine how well a book about Princess Di going through menopause would sell!

Dear Diary: Today Brian sent me a newspaper clipping which explained the similarity between raccoons and intellectual women: "They were both amusing for a while but soon became randomly vicious and learned how to open the refrigerator."

I'd be insulted except I know he doesn't think I'm intellectual.

Dear Diary: Someone should revive the old television show, *Queen for a Day*, which was so popular in the 1950s. The format includes confessions from self-sacrificing women who compete for the audience's sympathy by revealing the most intimate details of their personal lives. The one with the most pathetic story wins a major home appliance.

A 1990s pilot episode could feature, for example, a woman who hadn't dated in eighteen months, a professional woman who slept with her boss but wasn't promoted, and a mother whose only child had scored so low on his SATs that he was forced to attend a vocational school. I wonder who'd win.

Dear Diary: Love is not only blind, sometimes it's also deaf and dumb, and it doesn't always smell so good either...

A Bro' Grimm Fairy Tale

Little Black Fighting Hood

Destinee Worthington grew up in a small village a few miles south of Cleveland, Ohio. She was a pretty, peppy young woman who loved cheerleading and *The Cosby Show*. All her life, Destinee wanted to do only three things: date a famous heavyweight boxing champion, be crowned Miss America, and bring peace and harmony to the world.

Once a week, Destinee would take a train into the city to visit her grandmother. She always brought along a basket of food, pills for her grandmother's high blood pressure, and a copy of *TV Guide*. She visited on Thursday because Destinee and her grandmother liked to watch *The Cosby Show* together.

One Thursday, Destinee took a shortcut from the train station to her grandmother's apartment building. She walked through the lobby of the Ramada Inn, where a man approached her. Though he wasn't very tall, he had the solid build of a boxer. "Yo, mama," he said, looking her over, "where're you going in that cheerleading outfit?"

"I'm going to visit my grandmother," replied Destinee. "She lives all alone and I'm bringing her these White Castle burgers and her medication. She prefers Big Macs, but my best girlfriend works at White Castle."

"I like McDonald's better, too," said the man. "Maybe I'll pay a visit to your grandmother one of these days. Where does she live?"

Destinee, who was very naive, told the man her grandmother's address.

He just grinned. "Did anyone ever tell you that you look a lot like Robin Givens?" he asked and then ran out of the lobby. He made a quick stop at McDonald's and then raced over to the grandmother's house and knocked on the door.

"Who's there?" asked the old woman.

"It's me, Destinee," said the man, disguising his voice. "I've brought your medicine and a Big Mac."

Opening the door, she said, "Oh goody, a Big Mac," and before she could say anything more, the man grabbed Destinee's grandmother and locked her in the hall closet with the bag of Big Macs. From inside the closet, the man could hear the grandmother yell, "Hey! Where's the ketchup?" For a while she continued to complain. "These fries are cold!" she said several times, but before long, she ate all the food and fell asleep.

Destinee, who had dawdled in the ladies' room at the Ramada Inn trying to see any resemblance to Robin Givens, arrived at her grandmother's apartment a short time later.

When she knocked on the door, the man covered his head with a quilt, jumped in the grandmother's bed, and said (in a high-pitched voice), "Come in, dear, the door's open."

Destinee entered the apartment and skipped over to her grandmother's bed. "Watch this, grandmother," she said and performed a new cheer called "Push 'em Back!"

The man applauded wildly.

Destinee jumped out of her split and grabbed the man's hand. "What, grandmother, what big hands you have!" she said, a bit breathlessly.

"The better to embrace you with," said the man, giving Destinee a hug.

Destinee was surprised by the intensity of the hug, since her grandmother was usually rather frail. "Why, grandmother, what big ears you have."

"The better to hear you cheer!" said the man.

"Why grandmother, what big eyes you have."

"The better to see you jump in the air!" the man said.

Destinee was beginning to feel a little confused. "Why, grandmother, what big lips you have!"

"The better to kiss you." And, with that, the man grabbed Destinee and kissed her.

Destinee told him to stop, but he didn't. She struggled to get away, but he easily overpowered her.

"I'm Little Black Fighting Hood," the man told Destinee when he was ready to leave the apartment, "and if you tell anyone what happened today, you'll never cheerlead in this town again."

Destinee was very frightened, but she was also very brave, so the next day she went to the police and told them about Little Black Fighting Hood. The police arrested the man, and he was brought to trial. Now Little Black Fighting Hood is known as prisoner No. 765449 and spends his days in a prison in Illinois.

Destinee appeared on TV with Barbara Walters and on some other shows but found it very upsetting to keep repeating her story. She would like to put the incident far behind her, but in her heart, she knows that for the rest of her life, no matter what else happens, she'll always be known as the woman who got raped by Little Black Fighting Hood or, worse, as the bitch who had sex with him and then lied to everyone.

Meanwhile, in prison, Little Black Fighting Hood still doesn't understand why he got punished, although aside from the food, his life isn't all that bad. He works out every day and is getting stronger than ever. He's considered something of a hero among his cellmates, many of whom feel he got a bum rap.

When Little Black Fighting Hood gets out of prison, his boxing matches are expected to quadruple in ticket sales.

Nice Guys vs. Bad Boys

Keeping Score

There are only two kinds of men in this universe: Nice Guys and Bad Boys. Nice Guys are kind, attentive, and devoted. Bad Boys are aloof, selfish, and unreliable. As a general rule of thumb, we date Nice Guys but we fall for Bad Boys.

Why are we drawn to Bad Boys? The answer is revealed in the following chart, which analyzes and assigns points to the behavior patterns of both Nice Guys and Bad Boys.

It should be noted, by the way, that Bad Boys can be found in all age groups, from toddlers to old men, races, religions, colors, creeds, and neighborhoods.

NICE GUYS	BAD BOYS
Calls every day	Calls once every 2 weeks
Score: − 10 for being desperate	+ 10 for ever calling

Makes date 2 weeks in advance − 10 for being too available	Calls at last minute for date + 10 for being popular
Has steady job (accountant, dentist, etc.) − 10 for being ordinary	Unemployed + 10 for creativity, being artistic, anti-establishment
Wants to meet your best friend − 10 for trying to toady his way into your life	Wants to date your best friend + 10 for making you jealous
Wants a serious relationship − 10 for not finding one	Can't make a commitment + 10 for being a challenge
Works hard to please you − 10 for being dependent	Only pleases you when he feels like it + 10 for independence
Takes you to expensive restaurants − 10 for making you wear panty hose	Wants you to cook for him + 10 for eating your food
Extremely interested in your work − 10 for asking too many questions	Extremely interested in his work + 10 for making you into a good listener

Talks about his feelings − 10 because his feelings are never in sync with yours	Never discusses his feelings + 10 for allowing you to fantasize how he feels about you
Brings you roses − 10 for making you feel guilty for accepting gifts	Never promised you a rose garden + 10 for honesty
Always dresses neat and clean − 10 for always wearing geeky jeans	Doesn't care about clothes + 10 for looking great naked
Tells stupid jokes − 10 for boredom	Tells stupid jokes + 10 for making you laugh

BONUS POINTS

+ 10 for always driving a nice car	+ 250 for always being a great kisser

TOTAL SCORE

Nice Guys: − 110	Bad Boys: + 370

Any questions?

Mating Rituals
of Homo Sapiens

The Atlantic blue crab is known to scientists as *Callinectes
sapidus* Rathburn…Females, as we have seen before, decorate their claws with a bright orange-red, which color is seen
only at the extreme tips among males. Since females wave
their claws in and out during courtship, it may be that this
dimorphism is a sexually advantageous adaptation. If so, it is
probably a very important one, since the blue crab is
believed to be somewhat color-blind.
                                —William Warner, *Beautiful Swimmers*

Brightly colored fingernails are also part of the mating ritual
for females of the species *Homo sapiens*, known to scientists as
babes, broads, and *chicks*. Apparently, females in ever-increasing
numbers, are relying on painted and polished fingernails to
attract the males of their species. Otherwise, how else could
scientists explain the rise of nail salons in shopping malls across
America?

Also in striking similarity to the female Atlantic blue crab,
these same babes, chicks, and broads wave their fingernails in
and out during courtship, especially after they've paid a fortune
for nail wrapping. And, most ironic of all, males of both the

Atlantic blue crab and Homo sapiens species do not generally react to this aspect to the mating ritual. Although not all Homo sapiens are technically color-blind, the vast majority are oblivious.

For this reason, a man will rarely notice when a woman adorns herself with a new dress or pantsuit. Ironically, though, men are extremely observant when it comes to women's undergarments. This is why your boyfriend or husband will always notice when you are wearing a new push-up bra or when you've put on panty hose instead of a garter belt and stockings. Even if you're wearing jeans and a knee-length sweater, your man will know the difference between when you're wearing your Lollipop cotton panties or that heart-shaped G-string he bought you for Valentine's Day. This is part of the mating ritual called the Clark Kent Phenomenon, whereby men develop a limited form of X-ray vision, enabling them to see under your clothes while, at the same time, not noticing the actual outfit.

Physical grooming is important in the mating rituals between men and women, and some are shared by both genders. The single most important significant attribute among the species is hair. This is why both males and females spend a fortune on shampoos, conditioners, gels, mousses, and sprays. They turn to experts for cutting, styling, and coloring, and spend a considerable amount of precious morning time with a blow-dryer.

Hair quantity is critical to both genders, especially as the species ages. While men undergo painful transplant procedures to replace lost hair, women suffer through equally painful electrolysis to remove unwanted hair. The strongest common bond between the genders is the universally acknowledged truth that both men and women are unhappy with their hair.

Personal grooming has undergone some radical changes in the history of mating among Homo sapiens. In the sixteenth and seventeenth centuries, for example, men wore the wigs, the powder, the makeup, and the high heels. But as time progressed, they realized that such courtly appearance involved a whole lot of time and effort to put together, so over the decades, men pared down their daily grooming routine to a shower, shave, pair of clean underwear, and gold hoop earring.

Meanwhile, men encouraged women to develop complicated hairstyles and elaborate makeup, and to wear uncomfortable clothes and shoes—styles and fashions that men had decided were arbitrary, time-consuming, unnecessary, and oftentimes painful to wear for themselves. As men became more and more comfortable with their appearance, women were learning how to balance themselves on high heels and navigate a flight of stairs while wearing a tight skirt. And by encouraging women to spend all that time getting dressed to go out, men were allowing themselves more time to watch television while complaining that women were so vain and slow.

The bottom line is that sexy clothes are uncomfortable clothes. G-strings have been compared to wearing butt floss, high heels generate lower back pain and leg cramps, and wearing a push-up bra is like resting your breasts on a shelf. Still, these are the clothes we wear when participating in the mating ritual known as dating.

Webster's New Collegiate Dictionary defines *date* as "*a:* an appointment for a specified time; *esp:* a social engagement between two persons of the opposite sex; *b:* a person of the opposite sex with whom one has a social engagement." Several gay and lesbian groups are protesting this definition, demanding that the dictionary be recalled on the basis that the term "opposite sex" is arbitrary and prejudiced. At a recent Gay Pride Parade in San Francisco, angry homosexuals wore buttons and T-shirts that read "Webster was *homophobic*—if you don't know what it means, look it up!"

A date usually begins with an introduction, because one of the fundamental rules of mating is that you can't date yourself.

Single people go to great lengths to meet members of their species. They congregate in singles-only clubs, drinking establishments, and pool halls. They go to boring parties and art openings even when they'd much rather be home watching reruns of *Thirtysomething*. They participate in political activities and volunteer for charities as part of the endless quest to meet other members of their demographic group. They take classes in drawing, French, and automotive repair. They join religious groups, group therapy, and co-op boards. They attend weekends in the Catskills. They learn to ski.

They buy pets as an excuse to hang out at the local dog run, a haven for single people in most major cities. (Ironically, some people become attached to the pets once owned by former lovers. These are the most devoted pet owners as they share a common bond with their animal—both were abandoned by someone they loved and trusted.)

Once the male and the female have spotted each other, they emit a mating call meant to provoke more intimate contact. Most males of the species employ a provocative question to engage the female in conversation. The mating call of the 1970s sounded something like this: "What's your sign?"

The tenor of the call has changed considerably in the past twenty years to a much more declarative, sometimes accusatory, interpretation of this sound: "Have you been tested?"

If the female responds in a satisfactory manner to the male's inquiries, the pair engage in a conversation which can last anywhere from fifteen minutes to several hours. The object of the initial conversation is for the male to coerce the female into either meeting again at a specified time and place or agreeing to engage in sex within the next half hour.*

It is standard mating procedure for the male and female to have three meetings (aka dates) before engaging in sexual activities. Statistically, these meetings culminate in three meals, two snacks, seven cups of cappuccino, two to six long walks, four phone conversations, two movies (usually, one romantic comedy and one action-adventure), and one music-oriented event.

Following the initial sexual encounter, the mating will continue for a period of anywhere from two weeks to two and a half years, depending upon the quality of the sexual compatibility and a shared sensibility in the areas of economics and faithfulness.

The average relationship between the male and female lasts 825 days if the couple don't see each other all the time, or a total of 456 consecutive days and nights. According to the evolution of the species, as proposed in the late 1960s by Chuck Darwin, the great-great-grandson of *the* Charles Darwin and a former scriptwriter on *The Many Loves of Dobie Gillis*, the male and female can only be together for a certain amount of time before they drive each other crazy. In most cases, the relationship will only continue past the allocated 825/456 day formula if the couple has committed their names to a legal

---

*The later ritual, known as the *one-night stand*, has become increasingly rare; in fact, scientists at the Johns Hopkins Institute speculate that by the year 1995 the *one-night stand* may be totally extinct, except in certain regions of Nevada. For this reason, casual sex has been placed on the list of endangered activities, along with dates at the drive-in, becoming blood brothers or sisters, and men opening car doors for women.

document, has participated in giving birth to one or more children, or live in a rent-controlled apartment.

Single people have inhabited the planet since Adam and Eve. For this reason, scientists believe that single men and women will continue to populate the planet, and in all probability, will outlast the married counterparts of their species.

Ten Things You Should Never Tell...

Ten Things You Should Never Tell...Your Sister

1. When she was seven, you sold her to a neighbor kid for a quarter.
2. Mom always loved you best.
3. You hate the way she dresses.
4. Dad just lent you five thousand dollars for a new car.
5. You think her kids are spoiled.
6. People always ask, "Which one of you is the youngest?"
7. She was adopted.
8. You always wanted to be an only child.
9. Your boyfriend thinks she's far less attractive than you.
10. She's just like Mom.

Ten Things You Should Never Tell...Your Husband

1. His hairline is receding.
2. You sometimes think about having sex with someone else.

3. He always gives you a terrible birthday present.
4. His mother is on the phone.
5. Your mother is planning to spend her two-week vacation at your house.
6. He should stop at the gas station and ask for directions.
7. Your old college boyfriend asked you out to lunch.
8. You dented his car at the shopping mall.
9. You've been out pricing mink coats.
10. You didn't really have a headache last night.

Ten Things You Should Never Tell... Your Best Friend

1. Her diet isn't working.
2. Her boyfriend asked you out.
3. Her problems are stupid.
4. Her couch belongs on the far wall.
5. Your boyfriend thinks she's sexy.
6. Her apartment smells like a cat box.
7. She looks flat-chested in her new hundred-twenty-five-dollar swimsuit.
8. Your parents thinks she's a bad influence on you.
9. Her eye makeup is very dated.
10. Her dinner parties are boring.

Ten Things You Should Never Tell... Your Mother

1. You've had sex.
2. Your mother-in-law is a better cook.
3. You aren't wearing clean underwear.
4. You aren't wearing *any* underwear.

5. You're spending Thanksgiving with your in-laws.
6. You used to steal money from her purse.
7. You lied about the dog breaking her Waterford vase in 1968.
8. You don't believe in marriage.
9. Your new boyfriend is married.
10. You used to wish she was more like Donna Reed.

A User's Guide to Reentering the Dating Market

Single people slip out of the dating market for many social, economic, psychological, and ideological reasons including marriage, illness, bankruptcy, job promotion, exhaustion, and common sense. Inevitably, however, they return because of divorce, boredom, loneliness, and memory loss.

If you've been out of circulation for a long time, you will probably be feeling a little vulnerable and a lot anxious about dating again. You know you will be competing with women who spend several hours a week with personal trainers and two hundred fifty dollars for highlights and a henna. Women who live on Evian and Lean Cuisine.

The good news is that dating hasn't changed all that much since your adolescent years, which is, of course, also the bad news.

As you start dating again, you will be surprised to discover that all your wisdom and experience in the workplace and your confidence in building a stable family life count for absolutely nothing when you are waiting for a blind date to arrive. During general moments of stress in the dating process, you will return to the embryonic dating state which is best described as feeling like a self-conscious sixteen-year-old with bad skin and a beautiful sister.

Added to your basic insecurity is fear of the unknown, because dating today is a full-time job requiring more work than becoming a vice president by the age of thirty. Out there, in the condo down the block from your rent-controlled apartment, are women who think nothing of writing and answering personal ads, calling a man for a date, registering with a dating service, or asking all of their friends and family to fix them up on a blind date. In short, women who are practicing the guerrilla dating tactics of the nineties. It's time for you to join the rebel daters.

Topics to Avoid on a First Date

A first date is a special time when you and your guy will form your initial misconceptions about each other. You may mistake him for a potential husband; he may think of you as nonpossessive. In the days, weeks, and months to come, you will treasure these preliminary delusions.

However, this is no time to think about future. If single people required guarantees, they'd never go out with anyone. In the meantime, be happy. You have a date this month! To continue your streak, it is important to know what you can and cannot discuss on a first date.

Never, ever tell a man that you were dumped by your last boyfriend, husband, lover, or whatever you prefer to call him. This can only lead to a long, involved discussion that might make you cry and will certainly make your date feel uncomfortable. Also, many divorced women tend to turn vicious at the very mention of their ex-husband's name, especially when there are problems with the alimony payments (and when *aren't* there problems with the alimony?).

A weeping hysteric or an outraged martyr are not the images you want to project. If the subject of your past relationship comes up, tell your date that your former boyfriend or husband died. Even better, say he was killed in an avalanche while mountain-climbing in Nepal. This story may fulfill a sincere wish of yours; it will certainly make your ex seem a lot more interesting than he was.

Talk about him, him, him. Talk about sports, work, movies, or politics. In general, you should not be fooled into thinking that honesty is the best policy, especially on a first date. During this initial encounter, it is perfectly permissible to exaggerate, amplify, or overstate. Outright lying is also permissible. You want to make a good impression, so don't be yourself. Be smarter than you are. Be blonder. Be thinner. Be Diane Sawyer.

Date Rape

A word of caution needs to be said about date rape, which is a fairly recent concept to those who've been out of the dating market for the past decade or so. While date rape has been around for many centuries, it did not become a major television event until Patricia Bowman accused William Kennedy Smith of date rape during the Easter season in Palm Beach.

Date rape is difficult for a woman to prove because most juries assume that any woman who accepts an invitation from a man wants to have sex with him. Nothing could be further from the truth.

A man basically wants to sleep with any woman he finds attractive, and if it's a slow night, the not-so-attractive are also up for grabs. Therefore, men cannot imagine how little a woman wants to sleep with a total stranger. A woman can find all sorts of men attractive without wanting to have sex with any one of them. A woman doesn't want to sleep with a man until she has a full history of his past relationships; an idea of how he treats women, children, and small animals; his feelings about his mother; his shirt size; his plans for the future; and the way he operates a moving vehicle in bad weather.

In general (and I speak for my gender when I say this), women are much more interested in, and turned on by, a man's sense of humor, his intellect, his self-confidence, and his emotional capacity than by the size of his chest or other body parts. Obviously, this is a terrifying thought to any man *without* any sense of humor, intellect, self-confidence, or emotional capacity, which, coincidentally, describes most men who are guilty of date rape.

Tribal Dating Patterns

You meet for lunch on your first date. He calls two days later for a drink date.

Drinks go well. He calls five days later to ask you to dinner.

After dinner, you spend the night together. Even the awkward parts are fun. He waits ten days to call again.

You spend two nights in a row together.

He calls in two weeks, three days, and sixteen hours.

This tribal dating pattern is popularly known as Parry and Retreat.

After a great time together, he withdraws. The closer you get, the longer it takes for him to call again.

Just your luck. He falls madly in love with you and never calls again.

Evaluating Your Date

If you are not yet accustomed to the new dating experience, you may be confused once the evening has ended. How did it go? you wonder. Did I have a good time, or what?

Rule of thumb: Things went well if you managed to get through the evening without wanting to call your shrink, drink a pitcher of frozen margaritas, or down a Valium.

If your date really seemed to like you, you must try not to think less of him. If he calls to say how much he enjoyed himself, do not get nervous and tell him to drop dead.

If you see him again and begin to enjoy his company, you will probably be tempted to sabotage the romance as quickly as possible. (Best methods: being possessive, needy, and manipulative.)

Urban women like to rush through the initial happy/exciting/sexy part of a budding relationship in order to get to the misery and heartache stage as quickly as possible. If we had our way we'd probably skip the good stuff altogether—it's such a contradiction to our basic comfort level.

You Just Don't Understand Iron John

Communicating with Real Men!

Men and women speak different languages. She says Potato, and he says French fries. She says, "I need a new pair of shoes," and he says, "You just bought shoes last winter." She says, "We're having dinner with my mom this weekend," and he says, "I have to be in Philadelphia on Saturday."

Basically, men have trouble with conversations. You tell them how you feel, and they tell you what to do. Men hate to be helpless, so they try to solve problems. Women are used to being helpless, so they feel compassion for others in the same dilemma. A woman wants only for a man to listen to her and to empathize with what she's thinking and feeling. Unfortunately, men don't know how to listen unless someone is keeping a scorecard, tabulating statistics, or about to injure another person.

Women have this habit of thinking, thinking, thinking. They mull over every aspect of a situation to understand the source of their feelings and the root of the problem. They assume men do the same thing.

Wrong. When a man seems most lost in thought, what is he thinking about? Your relationship? Why you didn't return his last phone call? Were you flirting with his boss last week, or were you just being friendly? *Not.* He's thinking about how the Mets are going to do this season, or what he'll order from the menu, or what was on the flip side of the original recording of "In the Still of the Night." A woman can never understand a man's capacity to empty his brain of everything except what's happening in the next five minutes.

So, what do men think about? Nothing.

What do they want from women? Nothing more than what they've already got.

When will they change? Never.

Once you understand this basic premise, you can move on to the next big hurdle in the communication wars. Even when you have his attention, he never seems to understand a single word you're saying. You are a victim of vocabulary confusion.

See, men and women may say the same *words*, but in the gender-specific vocabulary of this decade, the opposing sexes define those words differently. In short, men and women speak the same language, but what they are saying to each other is entirely different.

For all of us who wish that men came with a decoder ring, here are some of the key phrases in the language of love, as interpreted by each of the sexes. Thus, the following is a *Lexicon of Love*—a dictionary to help men and women become functionally communicative in the nineties.

WORD	soon
Use in sentence	"I'll call you *soon.*"
Woman's Definition	2–3 days.
Man's Definition	2 weeks–next century

WORD/PHRASE	great date
Use in sentence	"That was a *great date*."
Woman's Definition	Flowers, nice restaurant, dancing, moonlight walk.
Man's Definition	Home-cooked meal, Charles Bronson videotape, sex.

WORD/PHRASE	best friend (same sex)
Use in sentence	"She/he is my *best friend*."
Woman's Definition	We share the intimate details of our emotional lives.
Man's Definition	We share the intimate details of our fantasy lives.

WORD	commitment
Use in sentence	"Yes, we have a *commitment*."
Woman's Definition	I won't look at another man.
Man's Definition	I won't talk about other women.

WORD	friends
Use in sentence	"Let's be *friends*."
Woman's Definition	We can go to dinner, but we won't have sex.
Man's Definition	We can have sex, but we won't have to discuss our relationship.

WORD	guys
Use in sentence	He says: "I'm meeting the *guys* for a drink."

Woman's Definition	He's going to pick up women.
Man's Definition	I'm meeting the guys for a drink and to pick up women.

WORD

busy

Use in sentence — "I'm *busy* on Friday night."

Woman's Definition — I'm washing my hair and doing laundry, but I want him to think I have date.

Man's Definition — I have a date.

WORD

feelings

Use in sentence — In any context.

Woman's Definition — Topic for discussion.

Man's Definition — A really bad song.

WORD/PHRASE

common bond

Use in sentence — "We share a *common bond*."

Woman's Definition — We have mutual interests.

Man's Definition — She enjoys baseball.

WORD

nice

Use in sentence — He says: "You look *nice*."

Woman's Definition — He hates my outfit.

Man's Definition — She looks nice.

WORD

forever

Use in sentence — "I'll love you *forever*."

Woman's Definition — Till the day you die.

Man's Definition — Till the sun comes up.

Rent-a-Date

Paid Advertising Supplement

Remember our company motto: *Don't call them gigolos, call them gainfully employed!!!*

The following is a small sampling of some of the more popular dates offered to our select clientele. Of course, for a slightly higher fee, we can tailor-make a date to fit your individual preferences. For example, we can provide a package that will include a long walk on a moonlit beach or slow dancing to Johnny Mathis records. (More sophisticated specialty services include the option of being stood up or embarrassed in a public place.)

For as little as $20!!! An intelligent man with a deep, sexy voice will call you on a Thursday evening and pretend to ask you out for Saturday night. During the course of the twenty-minute conversation, he will tell you how much he wants to see you, how much he admires your sense of humor, and that you are a hundred times prettier than your sister. For an extra fee, he will express interest in introducing you to his friends and family.

For a mere $50!!! A nice-looking man will arrive promptly at your house at eight o'clock, compliment you on your hair and outfit, and escort you to a movie theater where he will hold your hand in public. During the course of the movie, he will turn to you at least once and say, "My, I love that perfume you're wearing." While driving home, he'll solicit your opinion about the movie, which he will promptly agree is not only accurate but deeply profound and insightful. Upon arrival at your home, he will walk you to your door, tell you he had a lovely evening, and ask for another date. He will act crestfallen when you tell him that you cannot see him again because of religious differences. In vain, he will offer to convert.

The $75 special!!! A bearded artist type (chose from a painter, writer, actor, or advertising executive who writes screenplays in his spare time) will cook dinner for you in a downtown loft. After dinner, he will relinquish access to the remote control so that you can watch *Love Story* even if the Super Bowl is being broadcast. While watching television, he will rub your shoulders and ask for details of your day. He will be genuinely sympathetic to all your complaints and will never once accuse you of whining. When you are fully relaxed, he will either ask you to model for a portrait or reveal that you are the woman upon whom he has based the lead character in his latest novel/short story/screenplay. You will spend the remainder of the evening debating whether Demi Moore or Michelle Pfeiffer should play you in the movie.

A bargain at $100!!! A well-groomed professional (chose from a doctor, lawyer, dentist, or plumber) will wear a suit and tie and escort you to your mother's house for dinner, a family wedding, or your high-school reunion. At least once during the course of the evening, he will turn to the person of your choice, point to you, and say, "Isn't she magnificent? God, I wish she'd marry me!"

The $500 around-the-world special!!! A handsome man, at least ten years your junior, will sit next to you on an airplane and talk about his emotions, his childhood, and his need to find someone with whom he can spend the rest of his life. He will listen attentively to your advice and opinions. He will be fascinated by your life story and encourage you to express your feelings. When you tell him about the death of your favorite household pet, he will shed real tears. Upon arrival at your destination he will carry all your luggage, find a cab, and escort you to your hotel. Then he will go shopping with you, enjoying himself while you model an endless parade of outfits in front of him. He will offer to hold your pocketbook without complaining. Over a candlelight dinner that evening, he will confess that he's fallen madly in love with you and then insist you're crazy when you say he's too young for you. He will spend the rest of the evening telling you that age isn't important and that you look fifteen years younger than your actual age. He will make the point by favorably comparing you to every other woman in the restaurant.

For an additional $1,000, any of the above escorts will also beg to father your child. Upon being rejected, he will vow never to look at another woman again.

So, call us today!!!
Be the first in your co-op to actually have a date this weekend! As the president of the company, Marla Mahogany says, "I'm not just the Rent-a-Date president, I'm also dateless and desperate. If it weren't for this company, my neighbors would think I was gay."

Women's Studies
Further Reading

Good news for women! The bestseller lists are overflowing with important new books on women's issues.

The following list represents only a small sampling of new titles we highly recommend for women interested in politics, feminism, sexuality, feminist sexual politics, political sexism, the sexuality of feminist politics, radical feminism, radical sexual political feminism, and life-styles of the rich and famous.

You'll Never Eat Lunch in My House Again!
by Julia Philistine

In excruciating detail, Philistine reveals every drug she ever put down her throat, up her nose, or into her arm. Coughing up pieces of her hash pipe screen, Philistine teaches us how to cook heroin, smoke cocaine, and have sex in a drug-induced stupor while negotiating a major-motion-picture deal. Along the way, the author trashes every family member, friend, or colleague who ever befriended or worked with her. *You'll Never Eat Lunch in My House Again!* demonstrates that women can be just as sleazy and exploitative as men, and that although we've come a long way, baby, we haven't always gone in the right direction.

FAX: The Novella
by Nora Jean Baker

Sending transmission...Robin and Pat, two strangers of indeterminate gender, meet through a (900) FAX-DATE number.

Their relationship begins with a few brief question-and-answer notes. "I'm a Leo, what're you?" Pat inquires. "I'm a lefty," responds Robin, "but my sun also rises."

The correspondence soon blossoms into two-page (including cover sheet) declarations of esteem and then steams up once the couple discover a mutual proclivity for dirty limericks and double entendres. Before long, Pat and Robin realize that sex by fax is the safest sex there is. An intimate faxual relationship soon develops.

Then one day, Robin inadvertently transmits a fax meant for another paramour, and within hours, receives a fax from Pat's lawyer, suing for faxual infidelity.

The case gets faxed all the way to the Supreme Court, which finally rules that even though the couple never actually had physical contact, under the guidelines as set forth by the Congressional Subcommittee on Alternative Partnering, their fax correspondence constitutes a viable 1990s relationship.

A settlement is eventually reached. Robin's fax machine is impounded for a period of eighteen months.

Through an advertisement in a computer dating magazine, Pat eventually finds love and happiness with a modem mate...End of transmission.

Me, Me, Me
by Katharine Heartburn

Heartburn, long an idol of independent women, shows that though she's a talented star of stage and screen, she's not much of a writer. Her prose is sappy and her stories are superficial and less than insightful. *Me, Me, Me* will help dispel the image of Heartburn as the woman who can do everything, which should come as a relief to her more envious fans.

The Six Habits of Highly Defective People
by Stephen Convoy

We all know people we would describe as highly defective. Some of us are, in fact, married to such people, while others are "just good friends" with them.

Naturally, we can't help but wonder why some defective people succeed brilliantly in life. For the first time, psychologist and harmonica virtuoso Stephen "Big Lips" Convoy examines the inherent characteristics of defective people and points out how we can recognize them in corporate corridors and singles bars.

In stunning paragraphs and cunning little sentences, Convoy reveals the six most common habits of defective people: (1) name-dropping, (2) a penchant for daytime television, (3) over-accessorizing, (4) the compulsion to finish other people's sentences for them, (5) the desire to hunt down and kill small animals, (6) the belief in the superiority of any particular race, color, religion, creed, or fashion designer.

13,000 Reasons to Be Unhappy
by Betty Barbara Biffer

This companion volume to 9,000 *Reasons to Be Happy* was written just after the author quit smoking cigarettes. Items include varicose veins, Marilyn Quayle, traffic jams, step class, humidity, mammograms, automatic seat belts, when the airport loses your luggage and you have to wear the same underpants for three days in a row, people who own fourteen cats, EST, sour milk, cancer, nuclear war, the last day of a vacation, clogged sinks, getting lost, unemployment, game shows, bad clams, bad breath, tests, when the hair on your legs is thicker than the hair on your head, when you're wearing your new suede shoes and it starts to rain, speeding tickets, insects, bloating, paper cuts, when the bulb in the bathroom blows at night and you can't replace it because it's too dark so you have to brush your teeth in the dark, AIDS, people who are always late, losing a Scrabble game to someone not nearly as smart as you, too tight pants, and much, much more. The book includes many blank pages so that readers can add their own personal items to the list.

What Becomes of the Brokenhearted?

In 1921, Sigmund Freud delivered a landmark paper to the Leipzig branch of his newly founded Psychic Analytic Institute. He posed two questions which were to revolutionize the way doctors viewed interpersonal relationships. "What do women really want?" asked the great father of analysis. "And what becomes of the brokenhearted?"

Over the years, the first question would be pondered, analyzed, considered, rehashed, rejected, and reconsidered. Even today, it remains something of an enigma. Many scholars believe that the question was meant rhetorically, and in essence, Freud was saying, Women, you gotta love 'em, they never know what the hell they want.

Others believe Freud was implying that what women want is sexual gratification but he didn't say so out loud because he was unable to utter the word "orgasm" without giggling. In his diary, Freud wrote he was hoping, when he posed this question, that someone in the audience would shout out, "Women want an orgasm from their sexual partners," and he, Freud, would only have to nod his head in agreement.

"Nobody opened a mouth," he later complained to Jung. "Not even to take a guess."

The concept of sexual gratification would have to wait several decades to be publicly acknowledged. It was not until Helen Gurley Brown published *Sex and the Single Girl* that Freud's question would be answered. (Brown had no problem saying the word "orgasm" in front of an audience. In fact, she built a career on her capacity to fit the word into every conversation.)

In time, almost sixty years after Freud posed the question, the scientific community would finally discover what becomes of the brokenhearted. In 1982, The Freudian Slip and Slide Institute released a newly discovered collection of correspondence between Freud and Marvin Finklestein, his second cousin from his mother's side of the family. Recovering from a painful love affair, Marvin had written: "I need your help. Since Delphina returned to her husband, I am desolate. Please tell me, dear cousin, what becomes of the brokenhearted?"

Freud telegrammed an immediate reply: "Dear Marvin. The brokenhearted move to California. I don't know why. Sig."

As soon as this telegram was published, the governing board of the Freudian Slip and Slide Institute funded a Stanford research study to determine the scientific basis of Freud's conclusion. Did Freud mean that the brokenhearted literally moved to the West Coast of America? Was it a metaphor? Speculation? A practical joke? Or was Freud trying to persuade his cousin to leave Europe? (In a diary entry, Freud once called Marvin "that unfortunate specimen of inbreeding who could sink the family's reputation. The poor boy is not only cross-eyed, he laughs two days after he hears the punch line.")

The study concluded that, whatever his motives, Freud was indeed accurate in his assessment. With a margin of error hovering around 27 percent, the Stanford study proved that 84 percent of the people who lived in California for less than five years had been certifiably brokenhearted when they first arrived.

In a follow-up poll, the brokenhearted cited numerous reasons for relocating: the mild weather, the scenic landscape, the friendly people, the outdoor life-style, the sexual freedom, the abundance of hallucinogenic drugs, and the generous welfare benefits. (The survey was completed before California's current budgetary disasters.)

Today, many brokenhearted people seek help at the world famous Betty Fjord Clinic, named after the famous Norwegian stateswoman and recovering NyQuil addict. As a young girl, Fjord had been stood up for her junior-high-school prom after she had personally handcrafted over a thousand tissue carnations. She never fully recovered from the teenage trauma.

At the Fjord Clinic, high in the Redwood Valley, the brokenhearted are treated with the dignity and respect they do not receive in their own hometown. Many of the people who work at the clinic are also recovering from a broken heart. "Moving to California is a helpful first step in the recovery process, and the clinic is the perfect place to begin," reports Sarah Struthers, a forty-seven-year-old nurse at the Fjord Clinic who moved to California from Pittsburgh in 1987 after discovering her husband was sleeping with his dental hygienist.

Treatment at the clinic begins with four weeks of total self-indulgence. Patients are encouraged to overeat, smoke excessively, drink, take illicit drugs, and engage in mindless safe sex with fellow patients and staff members. They are required to watch too much television. They are prodded into talking on the phone for hours. Groups are organized so that patients can spend whole afternoons rehashing their past love affair, reviewing each event that led to the dissolution of their relationship, and imagining what course of action might have prevented the breakup. Patients are forced to speak their ex-lover's name at least once every fifteen minutes. Visualization techniques are used so that patients can imagine their ex-lover having sex with his or her new partner. Patients are required to sleep at least eighteen hours a night and to take long naps during the course of their day.

Phase two of the treatment at the clinic involves joining several recovery groups, including Alcoholics Anonymous, Overeaters Anonymous, Smokers Anonymous, Narcotics Anonymous, Nappers Anonymous, Couch Potatoes Anonymous, Talkers Anonymous, and Being Anonymous Anonymous. Patients stay in their Anonymous programs until they achieve total perfection. Then they move to Los Angeles and sell the rights to their life story to a producer of made-for-television movies.

Like many minorities, the brokenhearted are politically active in California. They recently helped lobby for passage of new legislation to protect their rights. Thanks to their efforts, "failure to warn" legislation for the brokenhearted was voted into law last year. A staple of product-liability law, failure to warn means that manufacturers are required to advise consumers of potential hazards. Under this expanded law, a person can now sue a lover, spouse, or dating companion if he or she fails to give fair warning that the relationship could end badly.

Precedent for this legislation was set in Santa Barbara when Cassandra Hammond sued her ex-lover Reginald Sweeney for not advising her early in the relationship that he was still in love with his former girlfriend. After dating Cassandra for seven and a half months, Reginald didn't return any of the messages Cassandra left on his machine. Finally, desperate to see him again, Cassandra arrived at Reginald's house on a Saturday morning where she discovered he was living with his ex-girlfriend, Laureen Barrister.

Under cross-examination by Cassandra's lawyer, Reginald confessed he'd often fantasized about Laureen while having sex with Cassandra. The foundation of his defense was that he'd never said he loved Cassandra and was therefore under no obligation to be faithful. The judge ruled that after seven and a half months of continuous dating, a woman has the legal right to assume her lover is either halfway in love with her, or at the very least, leaning towards what the judge termed a "love/commitment/possibility of a future direction."

After the jury returned a verdict of guilty, the judge struggled with his sentencing, denying Cassandra's request for castration as cruel, unusual, and slightly excessive punishment. "Only two things will actually make Cassandra feel better: time and falling in love with someone else. Unfortunately, the court is powerless to grant either of these contingencies," the judge declared, before awarding Cassandra the use and custody of Reginald's condom supply for six months. The case is currently on appeal based on new evidence, tape recordings of Reginald allegedly telling Cassandra he was sorry, he never meant to hurt her.

It is unlikely that Reginald's appeal will reverse the court's decision, even if the tape recording is entered as evidence. The "never meant to hurt" appeal, which male defendants have repeatedly invoked when forced to justify their actions, has been unilaterally rejected by every court of appeals, especially since more and more women have been appointed judges in California. In ever-increasing numbers, male defendants are being held accountable for their treatment of women in the area where they are most vulnerable: their finances.

In lieu of being able to provoke an emotional response from men, women are demanding financial compensation for emotional trauma. For this reason, community-property settlements have been expanded to include couples who live together, couples who've had a child together, and couples who've dated each other. Increasingly, the courts are being flooded by lawsuits for emotional distress caused by getting rejected after three dates or being abandoned at a rock concert or cocktail party.

While community-property laws dictate that spouses will be granted half the couple's holdings, the law now also provides that distressed daters will be given fractions of the defendant's estate. Plaintiffs often win a driveway or toolshed in their settlements. Recently, the courts awarded the front porch of a Victorian house to a party involved in a one-night stand in San Francisco.

Psychoanalysts have studied the legislation and treatment programs of the brokenhearted in California to understand better Freud's theories and his unanswered questions. Analyzing the accumulated data, as well as the legislation and pending court cases of the brokenhearted, the medical profession has concluded with certainty that what women really want is revenge.

Afterword

I Am Woman, Hear Me Snore!

One Sunday this summer, I was on a plane to California when I turned to the Book Review section of the *New York Times* and there, on the front page, was a long review of a nonfiction book called *I'm Dysfunctional, You're Dysfunctional*, by Wendy Sanders. It was a serious book that proposed everyone in our society was either in recovery or in denial.

Later, after landing in Los Angeles, I attended a convention of the American Booksellers Association, where I discovered another nonfiction title, *Happiness Through Superficiality*.

Also on view among the scholarly books was *The Madonna Connection: Representational Politics, Subcultural Identities and Cultural Theory*, a 322-page collection of essays that invoke Kant, Barthes, Foucault, and Brecht to explain the popularity of Madonna. Treatises include "Feminist Politics and Post-Modern Seduction: Madonna and the Struggle for Political Articulation" and "Material Girl: The Effacements of Post-Modern Culture." One scholar in the book claims that in watching Madonna's "Open Your Heart" video, "we can't help but notice suspiciously academic references to Lacan's essays about 'The

Gaze,' Deleuze and Guattari's 'Anti-Oedipus,' the feminist critique of woman's film image, and other citations too scholarly to be believed but too precise to be dismissed."

Now, I began to wonder if this was a conspiracy against humor writers. I mean, if people are going to start buying these titles for information, then what will they purchase for amusement?

The question became even more relevant to me a few weeks later, after I'd returned home and began a major effort to complete this book before my October 1 deadline. On September 3, I finished writing the preceding chapter, "What Becomes of the Brokenhearted?" Originally, I started with this idea: "Legal Aid for Bummer Dates." I tried to imagine what would happen if single people could sue each other for getting stood up or otherwise annoyed by people they were dating. As a flight of fancy, I concocted a system whereby the brokenhearted could be financially compensated. I was pleased with the finished chapter and not-so-humbly thought I'd been rather original in its conception and execution.

I mention I finished the piece on September 3 because on September 11, I opened the *New York Times* to discover this headline: "LAWYER, HEREAFTER BROKEN HEART, SUES TO MEND IT." The story, filed on September 5 by David Margolick, concerned a forty-four-year-old corporate lawyer from Chicago named Frank D. Zaffere III, who had filed suit against his twenty-one-year-old girlfriend of nine months, Maria Dillon, for breaking off their engagement. Mr. Zaffere was demanding that Ms. Dillon reimburse him for the $40,310 he spent wooing her. He had calculated the amount by adding up the cost of a fur coat, car, typewriter, engagement ring, bottle of champagne, and other miscellaneous items such as interest fees and court costs. He was further demanding the return of a $23.95

umbrella, a $22.00 red sweater, and a $7.99 Patsy Cline cassette.

Three days before filing the lawsuit, Mr. Zaffere offered to drop the charges if Ms. Dillon would agree to change her mind, pledge her faithfulness and truthfulness, and marry him within forty-five days. One lawyer advised Ms. Dillon to marry Mr. Zaffere and then divorce him. Ms. Dillon rejected the advice and found another lawyer. She claims to have spent a year's tuition on lawyer's fees. Ms. Dillon, a hostess in an Italian restaurant, is saving money so that she can attend law school. According to the *Times* article, the lawsuit has given Ms. Dillon "sleepless nights, prompted her to think of leaving Chicago, and driven her back to cigarettes. Also she has stopped dating."

Well sure, wouldn't you?

But that's not the point I'm stressing here. It's this life-imitating-art phenomenon that is so disconcerting to me. In writing, I'm always trying to get things to come out funny because real life is so dead serious. I thought I was being original; I thought I was being literally absurd. I forgot I was writing about the legal system.

My Aunt Hannah, may she rest in peace, used to mutter this Yiddish curse whenever she was upset, which roughly translated means "Your life should be filled with lawyers!" And then she would spit three times. Like many members of my family, she was a colorful character, but you wouldn't want to sit next to her at the dinner table.

We live in a litigious society, and as real life becomes ever more absurd, it gets increasing difficult to concoct anything that doesn't really happen. For example, a week ago, in this year's New York Democratic primary, I cast my vote for a dead man. Ted Weiss died a day before the election, and I not only voted for him, it was the first time in several elections that I voted without a hint of indecision. Apparently, I was not alone. The recently deceased Weiss won by an overwhelming majority.

Can you imagine how bad his opponent must feel? It's one thing to lose an election, but to lose to a dead man must be especially humiliating, not unlike many aspects of being single and dating in our society.

And yet despite the angst, we continue to date and to hope that some time, somewhere, we'll meet that special someone who'll come into our lives and end our dating career. We know this is possible because it's actually happened to our friends, our relatives, and the woman who used to live down the hall in apartment 4C.

As little girls we sang, "Someday My Prince Will Come" and took the words to heart. But, then, so did Princess Di, and look where it got her. Go know.